LOG IN TO ENGLISH 4

Richmond PUBLISHING

Scope & Sequence

		FUNCTION	GRAMMAR	LEXIS	RECYCLING
WELCOME					
L1	p.4	Talking about past events of one's life.		Extreme sports' equipment	Past simple & comparative forms
L2	p.6	Talking about future predictions.		Adjectives	Future predictions with *will* & *might* Adjectives with *-ed* & *-ing* Gerunds
UNIT 1		Mind what you do			
L1	p.8	Talking about life experiences.	Present perfect (aff.) for past experiences Past participles (reg. & irreg.)	Verb expressions	Action verbs Activities Adjectives
L2	p.10	Asking & answering about past experiences.	Have you ever...? Short answers Past participles (irreg.)	Verbs	Past tenses Adjectives
L3	p.12	Making recommendations.	*Should / shouldn't* *Must / mustn't* *It's (not) a good idea...*	Teen jobs	*Should* & *Must*
L4	p.14	Reading job ads & completing an application form.	Present perfect vs. Past simple	Jobs & related words	Past simple Present perfect Adjectives

Review Lesson Unit 1 **(p.16)** World Issues Magazine - WI1: *The rights of children*

		FUNCTION	GRAMMAR	LEXIS	RECYCLING
UNIT 2		Minds in conflict			
L1	p.18	Talking about recent actions.	Present perfect (aff., neg. & int.) for recent actions	Exclamations	Household tasks Verbs
L2	p.20	Talking about things you've done recently or haven't done yet.	Present perfect with *already* & *yet*		Family relationships
L3	p.22	Reporting news & talking about recent events.	Present perfect with *just*	Everyday objects In the news: verb + noun collocations	Objetcs Dates
L4	p.24	Writing a news article.	Tense review	Newspaper sections	Present perfect Past simple Present continuous

Review Lesson Unit 2 **(p.26)** World Issues Magazine - WI2: *From generation to generation*

		FUNCTION	GRAMMAR	LEXIS	RECYCLING
UNIT 3		Keeping an open mind			
L1	p.28	Talking about teenage lifestyles around the world.	Adverbs of manner (reg. & irreg.)	Adverbs	Countries Present simple Adjectives
L2	p.30	Talking about different teenage behaviors.	Comparative form of adverbs	Adverbs	Present perfect Past simple
L3	p.32	Talking about things in the past.	*Used to* (aff. & neg.)	Teen types Clothes	Clothes Physical description
L4	p.34	Asking & answering questions about life in the past.	*Used to* (int.)	Household appliances	Comparatives Interests & hobbies

Review Lesson Unit 3 **(p.36)** World Issues Magazine - WI3: *Life matters* & *SONG*

		FUNCTION	GRAMMAR	LEXIS	RECYCLING
UNIT 4		Make up your mind			
L1	p.38	Talking about jobs & small businesses.	Present perfect with *for* & *since*	Work places	Jobs Present perfect
L2	p.40	Talking about unusual jobs.	How long + Present perfect	Jobs	Jobs Present perfect
L3	p.42	Comparing different jobs.	*Not as... as*	Adjectives for describing jobs	Comparatives
L4	p.44	Talking about jobs in the future.	Adjective + prepositions + noun/-ing	Adjectives	Adjectives *Used to* Comparatives

Review Lesson Unit 4 **(p.46)** World Issues Magazine - WI4: *Be what you wanna be*

		FUNCTION	GRAMMAR	LEXIS	RECYCLING
UNIT 5		My mind is made up			
L1	p.48	Describing people's physical appearance & personality.	*What + look like?* *What + be like?*	Adjectives for describing people	Adjectives
L2	p.50	Talking about body art.	Relative clauses with *who* & *that*	Designs	
L3	p.52	Talking about online magazines.	Relative clauses with *where*	Magazine sections	Buildings & places
L4	p.54	Describing people you like and admire. Writing about a hero.	Pronouns: *one, ones*	Clothes & physical appearance	Adjectives
Review Lesson Unit 5 **(p.56)**			World Issues Magazine - WI5: *Body image*		
UNIT 6		It's all in your mind			
L1	p.58	Talking about dreams.	Pronouns: *somebody / someone, something & somewhere*	Sleep & dreams	
L2	p.60	Describing dreams & nightmares.	Pronouns: *some, any, no + -body / -thing / -where & one*	Health problems	Narrative tenses
L3	p.62	Interpreting dreams.	Question tags		Questions
L4	p.64	Reading a biography. Writing about your dreams.	Possessive *'s* (sing. & pl.)		Past tenses
Review Lesson Unit 6 **(p.66)**			World Issues Magazine - WI6: *Sleeping like a log*		
UNIT 7		Mind - boggling creations			
L1	p.68	Talking about modern technology.	Present passive (aff. & neg.)	Computer technology	Past participles
L2	p.70	Talking about the creation of video games.	Present passive (int.)	Video game production	Past participles
L3	p.72	Talking about famous inventions.	Past passive (aff., neg. & int.)		Useful gadgets
L4	p.74	Reading & writing about historical inventions & creations.	Passive voice with & without *by*		
Review Lesson Unit 7 **(p.76)**			World Issues Magazine - WI7: *To believe or not to believe? & SONG*		
UNIT 8		From mind to matter			
L1	p.78	Making plans & decisions.	*Going to & will*	School project materials	*Going to*
L2	p.80	Talking about future arrangements.	Present continuous for future arrangements	*Do & make* Chat abbreviations	Present continuous
L3	p.82	Giving advice.	*If I were you, I would(n't)...* *Ought to* *Should*	Multi-word verbs	*Should*
L4	p.84	Talking about imaginary situations.	Second conditional	Household gadgets	*Will* for predictions Comparatives The home
Review Lesson Unit 8 **(p.86)**			World Issues Magazine - WI8: *What the future holds*		

LEARNER'S LOG **(p.88)**
GRAMMAR LOG **(p.89)**
WORD LOG **(p.97)**
VERB LIST **(p.103)**
WORKBOOK **(p.105)**

Welcome Unit

Lesson 1

VOCABULARY WORK

extreme sports' equipment

1 **How many extreme sports can you write with these letters? Complete the first column of the table below.**

B I X C M R F D N G E T V U A S O K

SPORTS	EQUIPMENT
1 BMX biking	a bike, a helmet,
2 s	a wetsuit,
3 d	a wetsuit,
4 s	knee pads,
5 c	a helmet,

2 **What equipment do you need for each sport? Go back to #1 and complete the second column. Then choose TWO sports and write YOUR opinion about them.**

Example: I think surfing is really exciting but it is dangerous too. Surfers need to be very careful with the waves and the sharks!

1 ______

2 ______

READING

3 **Mat Hoffman is considered one of the best BMX vert ramp riders in the world. He is also the undisputed king of action sports injuries. Complete the paragraph using the *Past simple* form of these verbs:**

be become fall have invent make open produce publish start

M

Mat Hoffman (The Condor)

1 Mat Hoffman ______ born in 1972.
2 He ______ BMX riding at the age of 13.
3 He ______ a pro at the age of 16 (the youngest pro in the history of the sport).
4 In 1989, he ______ the first of a series of vert ramp tricks.
5 In 1991, he ______ his own bike and ______ his own business: Hoffman Bikes.
6 In 1993, he ______ a very serious accident when he ______ off a 21-foot ramp.
7 In 1995, he ______ the first film of a TV series for ESPN.
8 In 2002, he ______ his autobiography "The Ride of My Life".

LOG IN

4 **Practice with a classmate.**
In your notebook, write YOUR fact file. Write THREE true facts and THREE false ones. Take turns telling each other the facts and guess if they are true or false.

A I was born in May 1998. True or false?
B False! I know your birthday is in June.
A That's right and the year is wrong too!
B OK, now me. I broke my leg in 2007.
A I have no idea. Let me guess. True!
B No. I didn't break my leg, but I broke my arm.

5 **Read the descriptions and identify the superhero. Write [D] for Daredevil or [S] for Spider-Man.**

1 [ ] He is a Marvel Comics superhero created in 1964.
2 [ ] He is a Marvel Comics superhero created in 1962.
3 [ ] His public identity is Peter Parker, a newspaper photographer.
4 [ ] His public identity is Matt Murdock, a successful lawyer.
5 [ ] He became a superhero when he had an accident with toxic waste.
6 [ ] He became a superhero when a radioactive spider bit him.
7 [ ] His main characteristic is that he is blind but his other senses are superhuman.
8 [ ] His main characteristic is his ability to cling to walls.
9 [ ] He also has superhuman strength, a sixth sense for danger, perfect equilibrium, superhuman speed and agility, night vision and biological web-shooters.
10 [ ] He has a "radar-sense", acrobatic skills and special abilities in martial arts.

6 **Write sentences comparing Daredevil and Spider-Man using the adjectives below.**

1 strong Spider-Man is stronger than Daredevil.
2 powerful (sense of hearing) Daredevil's sense of hearing is more powerful than Spider Man's.
3 fast ______
4 good (sense of balance) ______
5 skilled (in martial arts) ______
6 famous ______

VOCABULARY WORK

adjectives

1 **Complete the crossword with TEN adjectives. The clues will help you.**

ACROSS

1. You can trust this kind of person.
2. This kind of person doesn't say much.
3. This person can be irritating.
4. This person loves adventure.
5. This person doesn't mind waiting for hours.

DOWN

6. This person is full of enthusiasm.
7. People are attracted to this person by his / her looks or personality.
8. This person is good at art.
9. Everybody likes this person.
10. This person loves going out and partying.

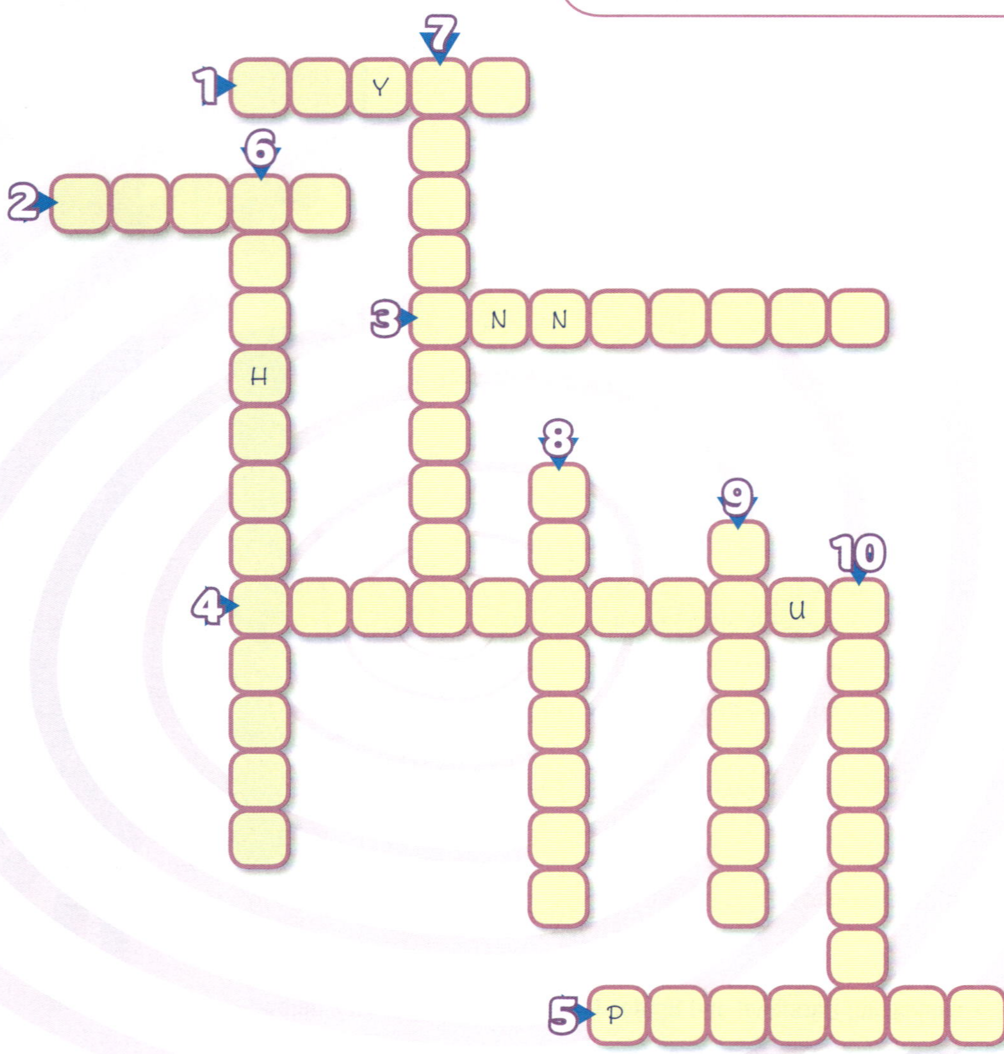

2 **Choose FIVE adjectives from #1 to describe YOUR friends and family.**

READING

3 **What does this text say about the future? Quickly read the article and check (✓) the correct alternative.**

1 ◯ Artificial intelligence will be a reality and robots will replace our friends.

2 ◯ There may be intelligent computers that will interact with us and respond to our feelings and emotions.

FRIENDS OF THE FUTURE?

After a long day at school, you turn on your computer to start your homework. An animated kid on your computer screen smiles and says, "Hi, it's good to see you again. But you look [1] **exhausted / exhausting**. Why don't you take a short break?" Does this sound like science fiction to you? Well, believe it or not, specialists are already investigating this area – affective computing. Scientists at the Massachusetts Institute of Technology (MIT) say that soon computers [2] **will / won't** recognize human emotions and respond to them. In fact, at MIT they already have the Learning Companion, a computer which has five different sensors:

1 One is a camera that focuses on your face. What does your expression say about your mood? Are you feeling enthusiastic, angry or [3] **boring / bored**?

2 A second camera tracks what you're looking at. If you [4] **look / will look** away from the screen, the computer will do something to get your attention.

3 There is a pressure sensor in the mouse. When you click the mouse too hard or too [5] **many / much** times, the computer senses your frustration and sends out signals for you to relax.

4 A skin sensor detects how much your hands are sweating. Palms which [6] **is / are** too sweaty may indicate anxiety.

5 And the fifth sensor checks your posture.

So you're probably wondering if this [7] **will / is** really work. [8] **A lot / A few** of people are suspicious. Sometimes it's hard for you to know how your best friend feels. If it's difficult for *us* to sense other people's feelings, [9] **teach / teaching** a computer has to be impossible!
But remember, technology never ceases to amaze us!

Now read the text again carefully and circle the correct options. Then listen and check your answers.

4 **Circle the correct options to give YOUR predictions about the world in 2030.**

1 Computers **might / will / won't** read our emotions.

2 Scientists **will / might / won't** clone human organs.

3 Gorillas **will / might / won't** become extinct.

4 Car accidents **will / might / won't** become more common.

5 People **will / might / won't** travel by teleportation.

Unit 1

Mind what you do

Lesson 1

VOCABULARY WORK

verb expressions

1 **Match the verb expressions to the pictures.**

- ◯ dye your hair
- ◯ ride a donkey
- ◯ shave your head
- ◯ eat worms
- ◯ sleep in a tent

2 **Which of the things in #1 would YOU like to do?**

READING & COMPREHENSION

3 (3) **Paul Scott is an adventurous 19-year-old from Vancouver. He is planning to trek across the Sahara desert. Read the newspaper article about Paul and check (✓) the correct option.**

Great ideas for great deeds

In the past five years 19-year-old Paul Scott has shaved his head, dyed his hair pink, slept in a tent in his garden, eaten worms, jumped out of an airplane, and now he is going to walk across the Sahara. No, he's not a crazy, rebellious teenager. He has done all these things for a very good reason – to raise money for cancer patients.

It all started when Paul was thirteen and his little sister, Ellie, was diagnosed with cancer and had to have several serious operations. She has been to the hospital lots of times. In order to help his parents with all the expenses, he decided to organize a fund-raising event with his classmates. They had a sponsored silence at school and for a day of silence they raised 832 dollars. This was when Paul realized that there was more he could do to help other people in need and since then he has organized a number of events.

His most recent challenge is going to take him and a group of friends across the Sahara desert.

"I have done many crazy things in my life, but I have never done anything like this before. In fact I have never been anywhere outside Canada so this is definitely the most challenging and exciting thing I have planned in my life! We're preparing to hike a hundred kilometers over dangerous terrain in boiling heat. I know it won't be easy, but it is for a good cause. We aim to raise at least $6,000 for cancer sufferers in Canada."

Stories like this bring hope to thousands of cancer patients and researchers.

Paul Scott wants to trek across the Sahara desert…

- ◯ as a personal challenge.
- ◯ to take part in an international race.
- ◯ to raise money for his sister's operation.
- ◯ to raise money for charity.

LANGUAGE LOGIN

Present perfect (aff. / never)

We form the Present perfect with *have* / *has* + past participle

I **have done** many crazy things.
He **has jumped** out of an airplane.
He **has eaten** worms.

I **have never done** anything like this before.
She **has never jumped** out of an airplane.
She **has never eaten** worms.

Regular past participles

jump → **jumped**
shave → ________
dye → ________

Irregular past participles

do → ________
drive → **driven**
eat → ________
go → **been***
ride → **ridden**
sleep → ________
take → **taken**
wear → **worn**

Tip

*When talking about past experiences, we use **been** as the past participle of the verb **to go**.
Check it out:
I **have** never **been** skydiving.
She **has been** to the hospital many times in her life.

Want more?

For a full list of irregular verbs, go to p. 103.

GO GET IT

present perfect / never

4 **Read the article in #3 again and find the *past participles* to complete the Language Login.**

5 **The article tells us everything Paul has done to raise money. Circle the things Paul *has done* or *has never done*.**

1 Paul **has** / **has never** shaved his head.
2 He **has** / **has never** driven a bus.
3 He **has** / **has never** slept in a tent.
4 He **has** / **has never** eaten worms.
5 He **has** / **has never** been abroad.

PRACTICE

6 **Read and complete the sentences that Paul's sister said about her family. Use the prompts. Follow the examples.**

1 ✗ ride a horse
I have never ridden a horse, but I would love to.

2 ✓ go skydiving
My brother has been skydiving.

3 ✓ go to the hospital
I ________ lots of times.

4 ✓ read
My family loves Harry Potter.
We ________ all the books.

5 ✗ travel abroad
My parents ________ abroad.

6 ✓ take a computer course
My Grandma ________ a computer course.

LOG IN

7 **Writing.**
In your notebook, write some sentences about things YOU and your family *have done* or *haven't done* during your lives. Use the verb expressions in #1 and the pictures for some ideas.
Example: I have slept in a hammock, but I've never slept in a tent. My brother has...

Lesson 2

READING & COMPREHENSION

1 **Read the postings below. Then check (✓) the correct option.**

PRESS THE REWIND BUTTON!

Have you ever wanted to press the rewind button? You know that feeling when you do something and then suddenly realize it was a big mistake? Don't worry! You're not alone! Let's take this opportunity to learn from each others' mistakes. Tell us about things you did, but soon afterwards regretted.

Message 1

posted by MC21 yesterday

I took a job as a babysitter. The baby was 6 months old. I knew I had to change his diaper but I didn't know how to do it. So I didn't. When his parents arrived and changed him, he had a bad diaper rash. I have felt sorry on different occasions in my life, but this time I felt sorry and embarrassed.

Cruel Martha

Message 2

posted by aoolalexis yesterday

I cheated on a test once. I usually don't cheat, I mean really cheat. I copied an answer from the person sitting next to me once. But this time I actually wrote the answers on my hand and the teacher found out. It was awful! I got a zero on the test and the school called my parents so everybody knew about it. I learned that day that it doesn't pay to cheat!

Ashamed Al

Message 3

posted by dan007 today

I lied to my parents once. You see, I wanted to go to a movie with a girl from class, but I knew my parents wouldn't let me. So I decided to invent a little white lie. I told them that I had to stay late at school to study with friends. To make a long story short, Mom and Dad couldn't find me and they were so worried that they almost called the police! I felt really bad about the whole thing and was grounded for a month! Lying to my parents was a bad idea. I don't recommend it.

Danny boy!

1 This text is...
- ◯ an article from a teen magazine.
- ◯ part of an online forum discussion.
- ◯ part of a personal blog.

2 It is about...
- ◯ mistakes people have made.
- ◯ naughty things people have done.
- ◯ crazy things people have done.

VOCABULARY WORK

expressions

2 **With the help of your teacher or dictionary, work out the meaning of the highlighted expressions in #1. Take notes in your notebook.**

LANGUAGE LOGIN

Have you ever…? & Short answers

Have you ever...?	Short answers
Have you **ever worked** as a babysitter?	Yes, I ______ . / Yes, lots of times! / loads of times!
Have you **ever done** something stupid?	Yes, of course I ______ . / Yes, once / twice / a few times.
Has Martha **ever dyed** her hair?	Yes, she has.
Have you **ever lied** to a friend?	No, I ______ .
Has Danny **ever been** grounded?	No, he hasn't. / No, never.

GO GET IT

have you ever…? & short answers

3 **Look at the Language Login. Complete it with *have* or *haven't*. Now, check (✓) the correct option.**

1 With *he*, *she* and *it*, we use…
- ◯ Have… ever…?
- ◯ Has… ever…?

2 We ask *Have you ever…?*
- ◯ to know about people's past experiences.
- ◯ to know about people's possessions.

PRACTICE

4 **Complete the dialogues below with the missing words based on the postings in #1.**

1 A ______ Martha ______ a diaper?
B No, she ______ .

2 A ______ Martha and Danny ______ on a test?
B I have no idea.

3 A ______ Al ever cheated on a test?
B Yes, he ______ .

4 A Martha, ______ you ______ sorry for something?
B Yes, ______ times!

Want more?
Complete the list of irregular verbs on p. 103 with these past participles: cut, made, said, sent, told, written.

5 **Use the verbs in the box in the correct form to write *Have you ever…?* questions.**

change	dye	tell (2x)	say	send

1 Have you ever told someone a friend's secret?

2 ______ your hair a different color?

3 ______ a white lie?

4 ______ a text message to the wrong person?

5 ______ a diaper?

6 ______ something horrible to a friend?

LOG IN

6 **Practice with a classmate.**
Ask and answer the questions in #5 using expressions from the Language Login.

A Have you ever told someone a friend's secret?
B Yes, I have. Once. / No, never.

Lesson 3

1 **Complete each sentence with the correct verb in the appropriate form. Then write YOUR answer for each question.**

be   do   look after   have   work

1 Have you ever ________________ small children?

2 Have you ever ________________ a headache?

3 Have you ever ________________ to get extra money?

4 Have you ever ________________ anything to raise money for charity?

5 Have you ever ________________ to a job interview?

READING & COMPREHENSION

2 **Read this magazine article about 16-year-old high school students. Write T for *true* and F for *false*.**

1 [ ] About a third of them work after school.

2 [ ] They work in order to help pay for their studies.

3 [ ] They work approximately two hours a day.

WORKING TEENS

In the USA approximately 30% of 16-year-old high school students think it is a good idea to have an after-school job. You may think these teenagers work for financial reasons, so they can help pay for their education, school books and things. However, statistics show that, in fact, most of these teenagers don't work because they need to. It is just so they can have extra money to buy things like designer sneakers and clothes that their parents won't pay for. On average, these adolescents work 17 hours a week and the most popular jobs they do are babysitting, pet sitting, dog walking, lawn mowing and yard work, household chores and cleaning, homework help, newspaper delivery and fast food work.

VOCABULARY WORK

teen jobs

3 **The article in #2 mentions different jobs that adolescents often do. Underline them and write the names of the jobs you can see in these pictures.**

dog walking

LANGUAGE LOGIN

Making recommendations

Read the *dos* and *don'ts* for a job interview.

DOs

You ____________________ wear professional clothes.

You ____________________ be enthusiastic.

It's a good idea to ask a few questions.

DON'Ts

You ____________________ use slang.

You **must never** chew gum.

You ____________________ arrive late.

It's not a good idea to appear uninterested.

LISTENING & COMPREHENSION

4 **Luke is sixteen and he's going to his first job interview. Mrs. Matheson is interviewing him. Listen to the interview and answer the questions.**

6

1 Which of these questions does Mrs. Matheson ask? Check (✓) TWO.

- ◯ Have you ever made dinner?
- ◯ Have you ever had a job like this before?
- ◯ Have you ever changed a diaper?
- ◯ Have you ever worked with children?

2 Which of the jobs in #3 is Luke having an interview for?

____

5 **Circle the correct options. Then listen to the interview again to check your answers.**

1 Luke is **late / on time** for the interview.
2 He is wearing **smart / sports** clothes.
3 He **appears / doesn't appear** to be interested in the job.
4 He **asks / doesn't ask** about his salary.

Now, do YOU think Luke got the job? Why?

GO GET IT

making recommendations

6 **Read the recommendations for job interviews in the Language Login. Complete with *should*, *shouldn't*, *must* or *mustn't*.**

PRACTICE

7 **Use the prompts to write recommendations for a student who is going to take an important test. Use a variety of expressions from the Language Login.**

1 stay up late studying the night before
It's not a good idea to stay up late studying the night before.

2 arrive late for the test
____

3 forget to write your name on the test
____

4 take one or two extra pens.
____

5 read the instructions carefully
____

6 check your answers at the end
____

7 **YOUR** idea
____

LOG IN

8 **Practice with a classmate.**
Ask and answer the questions.
Have you ever had an after-school or vacation job?
Is it common for adolescents in your country to have after-school or vacation jobs?
What recommendations would you give to a friend who wants to earn some extra money?

READING & COMPREHENSION

1 **Pablo is studying English at a language school where he saw these three job ads. Read the ads and sentences 1-5 below. Which jobs do the sentences refer to? Write A, B and C.**

7

A

National History Museum

We are looking for volunteers aged 14-17 to work in our museum.
You will interact with visitors to show the exhibits and tell foreigners about the history of our country. You will also assist children with craft projects, do face painting, and read stories. If you have worked with children, you are a good candidate. If you had good grades in history last semester, you also have a chance. Application forms with the secretary.

B

We need young people to work in our youth hostel. As this hostel is popular with young foreigners, English is essential. If you also speak other foreign languages this will really help. We need friendly, outgoing people to work at the front desk greeting visitors. You will also be expected to recommend places where visitors can go and things they can do, so it is important that you have a good knowledge of the city. Reasonable salary offered.
Call us at: 925-0704 or send an e-mail to youthadventure@poli.net.mx

C

Volunteers needed

Have you ever wanted to share some of your time with others? An international charity organization is looking for local volunteers to work on projects with street kids. This project started last year and we now have volunteers from many different countries, but we also need local people to work as translators. As well as taking part in activities at our centers, we will also expect you to help the foreign volunteers feel at home. Most of them have been with us for 2 or 3 months, so part of your job will be to take them to visit local places of interest and introduce them to local customs and food. We offer a small allowance to help pay for travel and food.
Interested? Call us now. ✆ 904-4556

1 It involves working with children. A and C
2 It involves taking people around the city. ______
3 You need to be good at history. ______
4 You will meet people from all over the world. ______
5 You will get a salary. ______

2 **Pablo decided to apply for one of the jobs in #1. He has to complete an application form. He has written some sentences. Check if they are right (✓) or wrong (✗). Make corrections when necessary.**

1 (✓) I'm very interested in languages and love learning about different cultures. ______
2 (✗) I never went abroad, but I read a lot about different countries on the Internet. never went abroad → have never been
3 ( ) I have only sixteen and so I have never worked before. ______
4 ( ) I am study English at the moment and I think this will be a great opportunity to get some practice. ______
5 ( ) I've had lots of experience with young children because I have four younger brothers and sisters. ______
6 ( ) I lived here all my life and so I know the city very well. ______
7 ( ) Last year I have helped organize a fund-raising event at school to help street kids. ______
8 ( ) I am very creative and one of my favorite subjects at school is art. ______

3 **Which job do YOU think he applied for? Why?**

______

LANGUAGE LOGIN

Present perfect vs. Past simple

Present perfect

I'**ve had** lots of experience with young children.
If you **have worked** with children, you stand a good chance.
Pilar **has been** a volunteer for two months.
They'**ve taken** 15 street kids to the museum.
Have you **ever wanted** to share some of your time with others?

Past simple

Last year I **worked** as a babysitter.
When did you **work** with kids?
She **started** working in a child care center in July.
Yesterday, the kids **did** a project during their visit.
Did you **apply** for that job you saw at your language school **last week**?

4 Look at the Language Login and:

1 complete the rules below with *Past simple* or *Present perfect*.

We use the ____________________ when we don't know when the action happened.

We use the ____________________ when there is reference to when the action happened.

2 explain why sentences 6 and 7 in #2 are wrong.

____

____

____

PRACTICE

5 Check (✓) the most appropriate option in each sentence.

1 Claire is very good at history. She ◯ **won** ✓ **has won** lots of prizes.

2 Jack ✓ **had** ◯ **has had** a job interview yesterday and he is now waiting to find out if he got the job.

3 I ◯ **never did** ◯ **have never done** volunteer work, but I'm going to start next month.

4 ◯ **Did you go** ◯ **Have you ever been** abroad over your last vacation?

5 How much money ◯ **did you raise** ◯ **have you raised** at the fund-rasing event on Saturday?

6 I was born in Rio de Janeiro and I still live there today, but I ◯ **never visited** ◯ **have never visited** the Sugar Loaf!

LOG IN

6 Writing.
Which job in #1 would be best for YOU? Why? Complete the application form. Use at least two sentences with the *Present perfect* and two with the *Past simple.*

Full name ______________________________

Address ______________________________

____

Date of birth ______________________________

What are your hobbies and interests?

____

____

____

Why are you interested in this job?

____

____

____

Tell us about any relevant experience you have had.

____

____

____

Want more?
Go to Grammar Log – G1 (p. 89)

1 Look at the pictures and prompts below. Make sentences in the *Present perfect*.

① Ruby / go abroad / many times

③ Susan / eat sushi / only once

② Mark / break his arm / twice

④ Nate / dye hair / three times

1 Ruby has been abroad many times. ______ Me too. / I haven't. ______

2 ______ ______

3 ______ ______

4 ______ ______

2 Now go back to #1 and respond to the sentences according to **YOUR** experiences. Follow the model.

3 A teen magazine is doing a survey on teen behavior. Complete the questions with the *Past participle* of the verbs in parentheses. Then check (✓) *Yes* or *No* according to **YOUR** experiences.

1	Have you ever ___had___ (have) a serious argument with a friend?	○ Yes	○ No
2	Have you ever ______ (stay up) all night?	○ Yes	○ No
3	Have you ever ______ (date) a boy / girl you didn't like?	○ Yes	○ No
4	Have you ever ______ (be) to a party without being invited?	○ Yes	○ No
5	Have you ever ______ (say) something horrible to a friend?	○ Yes	○ No

4 Now write sentences about **YOUR** answers in #3.

Example: I have never had a serious argument with a friend. / I have had an argument with a friend twice / many times.

______

______

______

______

5 ***Present perfect* or *Past simple*? Write sentences about YOU using the prompts below.**

1 a place you went to last weekend

I went to the movies.

2 a famous place you have been to

I have been to

3 a famous movie you haven't seen

4 something you did last night

5 something you didn't do last week

6 a sport you have never played

6 **Use one prompt from each column to write FIVE different sentences.**

Adults Teenagers Parents Students Teachers Children	must mustn't should shouldn't	listen to their children. respect their parents. cheat on their tests. smoke. turn off their cell phones in class. be late for class.

Example: Teenagers must respect their parents.

1 ___
2 ___
3 ___
4 ___
5 ___

7 **What about the things YOU *must / mustn't*, *should / shouldn't* do at home or school? Write FOUR sentences.**

1 ___
2 ___
3 ___
4 ___

Want more?
Go to Word Log U1 (p. 98)

Unit 2

Minds in conflict

Lesson 1

READING & COMPREHENSION

1 **Why do adolescents (aged 12-18) argue with their parents? A group of researchers in Australia investigated the causes and made a list. Read the list and check (✓) the THREE items that YOU think cause most arguments between teens and their parents.**

- ◯ appearance: clothes and hairstyle
- ◯ computer and video games
- ◯ eating habits
- ◯ getting up in the morning
- ◯ going out
- ◯ homework
- ◯ household chores
- ◯ loud music
- ◯ money
- ◯ telephone and cell phone bills

Adapted from www.aifs.gov.au

2 **Can YOU think of any other things that might cause conflict?**

3 **Now read the dialogues and match them to the pictures. Write 1-4. Which things in #1 are the causes of conflict in these four examples?**

8

1
Mom Oh look at you, Charlie. You haven't brushed your hair.
Charlie I have. It's just my new hairstyle.
Mom Oh. And have you brushed your teeth?
Charlie Mom. I'm sixteen, not six!

2
Mom Oh no! I don't believe it! She has turned up the volume again! You go this time.
Dad Okay. But if she doesn't turn it down, I'm going to take the stereo away from her.

3
Dad Charlie! It's 9 o'clock and you haven't done your homework!
Charlie Oh. Come on Dad! Just let me see the end of this program.
Dad No. It's late!

4
Lucy Mom. What can I have for breakfast? Charlie has eaten all the bread! There's none left!
Mom Oh Charlie. I can't believe you ate all the bread. You really mustn't eat so much. What about your diet?
Charlie But Mom I'm always really hungry in the morning!

A

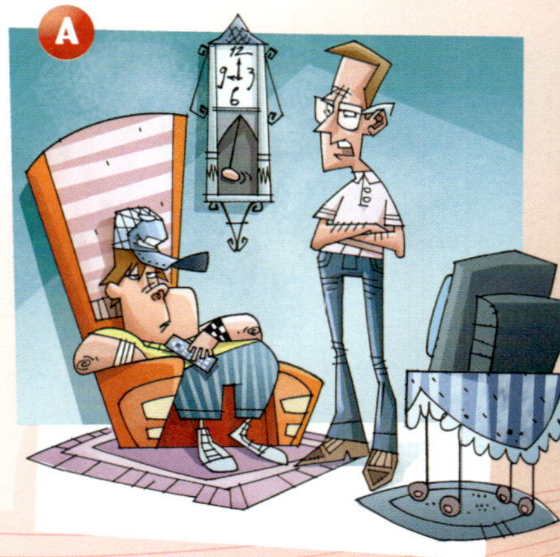

B

LANGUAGE LOGIN

Present perfect (aff. / neg. / int.)

We use the *Present perfect* to talk about **recent** / **present** actions. The result of the action is often visible.

Affirmative	Negative	Interrogative
You**'ve eaten** all the bread.	You **haven't brushed** your hair.	**Have** you **brushed** your teeth?
She**'s turned up** the volume.	He **hasn't done** his homework.	What **has** he **done**?

C

D

GOT GET IT

present perfect (aff., neg., int.)

4 **Circle FIVE examples of the *Present perfect* in the dialogues in #3. Then look at the Language Login and circle the correct option to make the rule.**

PRACTICE

5 **Write the *Past participles* of the given verbs. Refer to p. 103 if necessary.**

break ______________	fall ______________
cut ______________	be ______________
pass ______________	hear ______________

6 **Read these exclamations and complete the sentences about what has happened. Use the verbs in #5.**

1 "Oh dear!" She's heard some bad news.
2 "Help!" He ______________ in the river.
3 "Congratulations!" Her friend ______________ an important exam.
4 "Ouch!" He ______________ himself.
5 "Oh no!" She ______________ the teapot.

7 **Now talk about YOU. What have you done so far today? Use the prompts given.**

1 (take a shower)
I have taken a shower. / I haven't taken a shower.
2 (have breakfast)
____
3 (watch TV)
____
4 (clean your bedroom)
____

READING

1 **Read the quiz and complete the Vocabulary Box with the highlighted words.**

How often do you argue with your parents?

Too often, maybe?
Nowadays arguments between kids and their parents are common. Some say it's all part of growing up, but there are definitely ways of minimizing these conflicts and making your life easier. Answer these three questions and see if you are getting things right!

1 It's Friday night and you want to go to your best friend's party. All your friends will be there, but your parents say you can't go. What do you do?

a *Secretly leave the house. You will only stay there a few hours. Mom and Dad probably won't notice.*
b *Get down on your hands and knees, make a sad face and **beg**!*
c *Listen to your parent's side of the story and try to come to an agreement.*

2 Some new sneakers have just come out and you really want to buy them. Unfortunately you're **broke**. What do you do?

a *Get money from Mom's wallet. She will never notice.*
b *Ask your parents to give you a birthday present in advance.*
c *Volunteer to do some jobs around the house for some extra spending money and / or borrow the rest of the money from your parents.*

3 You and your parents have just had a big argument. You're so upset. You know you are right and they are wrong. But you are now **grounded** for the next week. What do you do?

a *Don't talk to or look at your parents for the next week.*
b *Scream, shout and **slam** the door after they give you your punishment, just so you can have the last word.*
c *Stop shouting. Suggest sitting down to discuss the issue like adults.*

Vocabulary Box

_______________ – ask for strongly, implore
_______________ – without money
_______________ – not allowed to go out as a form of punishment
_______________ – close with force, usually making a loud noise

2 **Now do the quiz in #1. Circle the correct answers for YOU. Then look at the key on page 21 and read about the answers that show good communication between teens and their parents.**

LISTENING

3 **Listen to Isabel and her mom. Answer the questions.**

1 What did Isabel want to do? _______________
2 Did Isabel get to do what she wanted? _______________
3 According to the quiz in #1, what did she do wrong?

____

____

LANGUAGE LOGIN

Present perfect with *already* & *yet*

Already

I**'ve already asked** you to clean your room three times.
He**'s already cleaned** his bedroom.

Yet

Have you **cleaned** your room **yet**?
He **hasn't done** his homework **yet**.

Attention!

Use ____________ in affirmative sentences and ____________ in interrogative and negative sentences.

Use ____________ at the end of the sentence.

Use ____________ between *have* and *has* and the main verb.

GO GET IT

already & yet

4 Now read the dialogue, study the highlighted words and complete the rules in the Language Login with *yet* or *already*.

Mom Have you cleaned your room yet?

Isabel No, I started to do it, but I haven't finished yet.

Mom Oh Isabel! How many times do I have to tell you to do things?

Isabel Oh Mom! I'll do it later, OK? Right now I'm going to the movies with Rod.

Mom No, you're not! You're going to clean your room right now! And then you can go.

Isabel But Mom, Rod's waiting for me. He's already bought the tickets! It's not fair!

Mom Listen, Isabel. I've already asked you to clean your room three times! You had all day to do it. Now go to your bedroom and stay there!

Isabel It's not fair. You always ruin everything!

PRACTICE

5 Make interrogative sentences with *yet*.

1 your sister / clean her room
Has your sister cleaned her room yet?

2 John / do his homework
____

3 you / study for the test
____

4 Grandma / got home
____

6 Complete the sentences following the model.

1 Roberta hasn't seen that movie yet, but Luke
has already seen it.

2 Susie has already made her bed, but Daniel
____

3 Chris hasn't had a shower yet, but Sally
____

4 I've already finished my homework, but my brother
____

LOG IN

7 Writing.
In your notebook, write a dialogue between a parent and a teenager involving a situation of conflict. Read the advice given in the answers to the quiz in #2 again so that you can decide how the teenager is going to act. Use the dialogue in #4 as a reference. Include examples of the *Present perfect* with *yet* and *already* in your dialogue.

QUIZ KEY:

Option C in the three questions shows a healthy way to communicate with parents.

1 Your parents don't want you going to places they don't know anything about. You have to show them you are responsible. Explain that you'll be home by the time they say. If this doesn't work, don't get angry. Start thinking about how to get to the next party!

2 When you volunteer to co jobs around the house, you show initiative. Parents like that! The second part to this answer is *borrow*. Don't immediately ask your parents for the money. Borrow some and prove you're the kind of person that pays it back. Then ask for more. Who knows you may even get more than just the sneakers!

3 When there is shouting, no one can hear what the other person is saying. Slamming doors is childish. A child shouting at a parent is disrespectful, so don't do it! When you talk to your parents with respect, you are more likely to get respect. Try to negotiate. Both sides should present their arguments and then hopefully come to an agreement.

VOCABULARY WORK

everyday objects

1 **How many of these objects can YOU name? Write the names under the pictures.**

1 

2 

3 

4 

5 

6 

7 

8 

9 

10 

2 **Who in YOUR family do you associate with the different objects in #1?**
Example: *a record player – my grandfather*

3 **What do YOU know about events from your parents' and your grandparents' lifetime? Read these news headlines and match them to the different years.**

1945 1953 1962 1967 ~~1969~~ 1982 1985 1997

1 **Neil Armstrong has just become the first man to step on the moon.** 1969

2 **The USA has dropped an atomic bomb on Hiroshima.** ______

3 The Beatles **have just released** a new album, *Sgt Pepper's Lonely Hearts Club Band.* ______

4 *The Live Aid* concert has raised almost 285 million dollars for famine relief in Ethiopia. ______

5 **A new female pop idol has hit the charts. Her name is Madonna.** ______

6 **Princess Diana has tragically died in a car accident.** ______

7 Brazil **has just won** the World Cup for the second time. ______

8 Edmund Hillary and Tenzing Norgay **have just reached** the top of Mount Everest. ______

GO GET IT

present perfect with just

4 **Look at the highlighted examples in #3. Then use those verbs in the correct form to complete the sentences in the Language Login.**

LANGUAGE LOGIN

Present perfect with *just*

Five criminals **have just escaped** from a California prison.

Madonna ______________________ a new album.

Lars Grael and Marcelo Jordão ______________________ a sailing regatta in Miami.

An earthquake ______________________ Mexico.

Attention! Use the *Present perfect* with **just** to talk about very recent events.

PRACTICE

5 **Rosie is a working mother. She was at work all day and has just arrived home. What's just happened in her home? Use the prompts to make sentences using the *Present perfect* and *just*.** **Refer to p. 103 if necessary.**

1 arrive home Rosie has just arrived home.
2 burn his finger ______________________
3 fall over ______________________
4 spill his juice ______________________
5 win a game ______________________

VOCABULARY WORK

in the news (verb collocations)

6 **Match the verbs below with possible collocations. One verb is not used.**

break catch crash discover elect get ~~release~~ win

1 ___release___ a new DVD, a film
2 ______________ an award, a medal, a competition
3 ______________ married, divorced, better
4 ______________ a cure, some dinosaur bones
5 ______________ a new president, a leader
6 ______________ a record, a leg
7 ______________ a criminal, a wild animal

LOG IN

7 **Practice with a classmate.**
Look at these pictures taken by photographers working for a newspaper and discuss with your classmate what YOU think has just happened.

A I think that in picture two a famous person has just got married.
B Yes, I agree. They have just had an amazing party and now they are going on their honeymoon.
C I don't know. I think this couple has just won a prize or something.

1 **Circle the correct option.**

1 A Let's go and see the new James Bond movie tonight.
B No, not that movie. I've **already** / **yet** seen it.

2 A What do you think of the new shopping mall?
B I haven't been there **already** / **yet**.

3 Can you believe it? Jake's only thirteen and he's **already** / **yet** passed the exams to get into college.

4 A How's Sandra?
B She's really well. Didn't you hear? She's **just** / **yet** got married.

5 What a shame you didn't come five minutes earlier. We've **just** / **yet** finished the cake.

6 A Can I have a look at the paper now?
B Sorry, I haven't finished reading it **already** / **yet**. Can you wait a bit?

Lesson 4

READING & COMPREHENSION

2 **Read these news stories from the year 2050 and answer the questions.**

11

July 12, 2050

MAIA X1000 RETURNS FROM TZALTA

The first aliens have just arrived on Earth. The NASA spaceship, MAIA X1000, landed in Houston early this morning after a very successful mission. A group of five astronauts spent more than three months in space studying life on Tzalta and they have brought back samples of plants and small creatures from the planet. Scientists are now studying these samples and hope that they will help reach more groundbreaking conclusions about life on different planets. The scientists and astronauts haven't given the public many details about their findings yet as they will need time before they are able to present an official report. However, they have revealed that the samples from Tzalta are very different to anything that exists here on earth. More

BRAZILIANS CELEBRATE THEIR TENTH WORLD CUP VICTORY

Brazil has just won the World Cup Final in Caracas. It was an extremely exciting game against the USA, and left spectators extremely nervous right until the very end. Two minutes before the end of the game it looked as if it was going to be a victory for the Americans, but then the new soccer superstar Paulinho scored a spectacular goal, making the final score a 2-2 tie. Much to the disappointment of the American fans, Brazil went on to beat the USA 5-3 in a penalty shoot out. At this moment fans are celebrating all over Brazil and, all over the world! Brazilians have taken to the streets of Rio de Janeiro, São Paulo and other major cities in celebration of their tenth World Cup victory! The Brazilian team has already boarded their plane to fly back to Brazil where a warm welcome awaits them. More

1 Are these stories telling good news or bad news? ______

2 Do **YOU** think either of these stories really could happen before the year 2050? Why? ______

GO GET IT

verb tenses

3 **Read the Language Login and then write one more example for each verb tense. Find your examples in the World Cup news story in #2.**

PRACTICE

4 **These are sentences from an American newspaper. Complete them using the *Present perfect*, *Past simple* or *Present continuous*.**

1 Scientists ________________ (discover) a cure for mysterious disease.

2 At the moment people ________________ (line up) to buy tickets for the opening performance.

3 Yesterday the people of Chile ______________ (vote) for new President.

4 The hurricane ________________ (approach) Florida now.

5 The World Eco Conference, which __________ (start) two days ago, ______________ (come) to an end.

VOCABULARY WORK

newspaper sections

5 **Read sentences from #4 again and match them to the appropriate newspaper section below.**

LANGUAGE LOGIN

Writing a news article – tense review

Present perfect: to introduce recent news and events.
Example: The first aliens **have** just **arrived** on Earth.

____

____

Past simple: to give details about what happened.
Example: The NASA spaceship, MAIA X1000, **landed** in Houston early this morning.

____

____

Present continuous: to say what is happening at the moment.
Example: Scientists **are** now **studying** these samples.

____

6 **Read the headlines of different news stories. Decide which story YOU think is most likely to happen by 2050 and which you think is least likely to happen.**

1 Twenty space tourists have just landed at Galaxia Space Station.
2 Scientists have just cloned the first human.
3 A huge tsunami has just hit the west coast of the USA.
4 A 30-year-old woman has just given birth to ten healthy children.
5 The people of Argentina have just elected their first black President.
6 A new fashion has hit the streets of New York – skirts for men!

LOG IN

7 **Writing.**
YOU are a journalist in 2050. Choose one of the stories in #6 and write a short newspaper article. Use the *Present perfect*, the *Past simple* and the *Present continuous*. Use the news stories in #2 as models.

Want more?
Go to Grammar Log – G2 (p. 89)

1 **Look at the pictures below. What has just happened?**

Faith has just hurt herself. (hurt)

Gabrielle ______________________________ (find)

Zac ______________________________ (receive)

Blake ______________________________ (win)

Jada and Rebecca ______________________________ (see)

2 **Look at Jenna's *to do list*. Write sentences about the things she has already done and the ones she hasn't done yet. Follow the examples.**

To do list

1 take the dog for a walk ✓
2 buy dog food ✗
3 download favorite songs ✗
4 finish project (science) ✓
5 phone Autumn ✓
6 get Mom's mail downstairs ✗

1 Jenna has already taken the dog for a walk.
2 She hasn't bought dog food yet.
3 ______________________________
4 ______________________________
5 ______________________________
6 ______________________________

3 **Read the magazine article below and circle the correct options.**

In February 2001, the life of Brazilian rock singer Herbert Vianna [1] **has changed / changed** forever. He had an airplane accident and [2] **has lost / lost** part of his brain capacity as a result. He was in a coma for a long time and spent 44 days in hospital. It was a miracle he [3] **survived / survives.**

Herbert is an example of discipline and perseverance. Since he left the hospital, he [4] **worked / has worked** hard to recover his health. In the beginning he couldn't remember people's faces or names, but after some time he even started playing the guitar and singing to the doctors, nurses and other patients! In June, only four months after the accident, he [5] **has gone / went** onstage to sing a song with Argentinean singer Fito Paez, his longtime friend. Since then, he [6] **performed / has performed** in many successful shows with his band, *Os Paralamas do Sucesso*, and has also started driving! He [7] **is still using / has just used** a wheelchair and he hasn't stopped his treatment [8] **yet / already**. We all hope one day he will be able to walk again.

4 **Read the text again and write T for *true* or F for *false*.**

1 [ ] Herbert Vianna has suffered severe brain damage.
2 [ ] He has completely recovered from the accident.
3 [ ] He can't drive anymore.
4 [ ] He can't walk.
5 [ ] He hasn't sung since the accident.

5 **Think about an event that changed YOUR life. Write about it. Use the questions below to help you.**

What happened?
When did it happen?
What is going on now because of it?

Example: I have just met my soul mate. We went to the same party last month and we are now going out together.

____

____

____

Want more?
Go to Word Log U2 (p. 98)

Unit 3

Keeping an open mind

READING & COMPREHENSION

Lesson 1

1 **Read the magazine article and match the texts and the places they refer to.**

12

~~Africa~~	China and Japan	Europe and the USA	India	Latin America	Russia

ARE TEENS THE SAME WHEREVER YOU GO?

TEEN CULTURE

[1] Africa
Although it is difficult for teens to find a balance among their three cultural influences – indigenous, European and Islamic – they deal well with globalization and their own traditions. Teenagers in those countries are emotionally African, but they try hard to hide their "Africanity" under modern values.

[2] ______
On one side there are the homeless children and on the other the millionaires from the Indian Silicon Valley (Bangalore). But the two extremes have the same national mentality. In both urban and rural areas, all around the country adolescents follow strong family values.

[3] ______
In those countries teens must adapt to an environment which is changing fast. The image of teenagers who are strictly controlled by their parents, have no social life and are completely devoted to their studies belongs to the past.

[4] ______
Teenage girls have to find their place between opposing social expectations: get married, stay home and raise their children or enjoy the freedom that comes from the emerging economy and westernization.

[5] ______
Teens have become less religious than their parents' generation. This is basically a consequence of the fact that the religious institutions in Latin America are badly connected to the teens' interests and problems.

[6] ______
In the developed West there is a pattern: teen girls and young women seem to be getting better academic results than boys and young men. But there is a general feeling that there are plenty of opportunities for everyone.

Based on *Revista Galileu* Jan 2006.

2 **Read the texts in #1 again and write T for *true* and F for *false*.**

1 [ ] There are big economical differences in India.
2 [ ] Chinese and Japanese teenagers have changed a lot lately.
3 [ ] Modern Russian girls must choose between traditional and modern values now.
4 [ ] Latin American teens have the same religious values as their parents.
5 [ ] European and American boys tend to do better than girls at school.

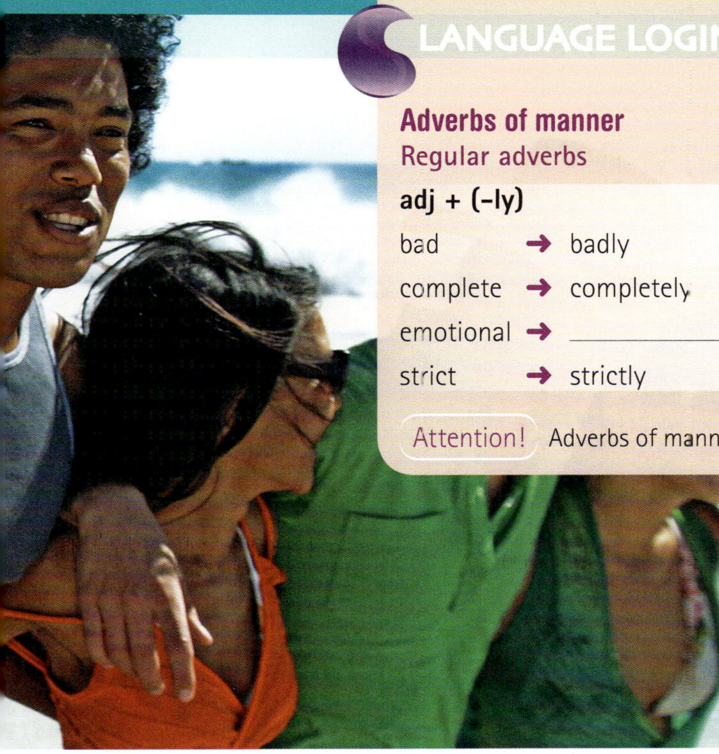

LANGUAGE LOGIN

Adverbs of manner

Regular adverbs					Irregular adverbs		
adj + (-ly)			**adj - (-y + -ily)**				
bad	→	badly	happy	→ happily	fast	→	fast
complete	→	completely	easy	→ easily	good	→	well
emotional	→	____________			hard	→	____________
strict	→	strictly			early	→	early
					late	→	late

Attention! Adverbs of manner describe *how people do things or how things happen.*

GO GET IT

adverbs of manner

3 Look at the highlighted words in #1, complete the Language Login and check (✓) the correct option.

The *adverbs of manner* come ◯ **before** ◯ **after** the main verb.

PRACTICE

4 Complete the sentences with the adverbs of the adjectives in parentheses.

WHAT DO ALL TEENAGERS HAVE IN COMMON?

1 Most teenagers have strong opinions and like to express them ____clearly____ . (clear)

2 Teenagers often stay up ____________ and get up ____________ . (late / late)

3 Most teenage boys like to express their emotions ____________ . (physical)

4 Most teenagers eat a lot because their metabolism works ____________ . (fast)

5 Teenagers are usually noisy and tend to talk and laugh ____________ . (loud)

6 Teenagers' moods usually change ____________ . (quick).

5 Do YOU have any of the characteristics as the teenagers described in #4?

6 Look at the pictures and complete the sentences with the appropriate adverbs in the box.

~~bad~~	early	fast	happy	late

1 Oh, no! He sings so ____badly____ !

2 The children are playing ____________ .

3 I think Thelma is going to win the race. She runs very ____________ .

4 Tom usually arrives late for class, but this morning he arrived very ____________ .

Lesson 2

READING & COMPREHENSION

1 13 **Read the book review on this bookstore webpage and check (✓) the appropriate answer.**

TEENS CATALOG

More details about this title

Price: $5.99

Rating: ☆☆☆☆☆

▶ Reviews and Rating

Anne Frank: The Diary of a Young Girl **by Anne Frank**

Anne Frank's *The Diary of a Young Girl* is one of best known documents of the Holocaust. Since its publication in 1947, Anne Frank's story has been translated into 67 languages and is one of the most popular books in the world.

The book tells the true story of Anne Frank, a Jewish girl who lived and died during the Holocaust. She and her family, along with four others, were forced to hide for 25 months in an annex of rooms above her father's office in Amsterdam to try to escape the horrors of Nazi occupation. Anne, who was only thirteen when she went into the secret rooms, kept a diary where she wrote about their hard life in the annex and the horrors of war. She also wrote about being a teenager, with all the difficulties and discoveries teenagers still face nowadays.

When Anne and all others were captured and deported to Nazi concentration camps, her diary was saved by a friend of the family. Anne Frank died of typhus at Bergen-Belsen concentration camp. She was only fifteen years old.

Read this book and find out from one of the most famous teens in modern history what it feels like to live in hiding in an occupied country.

Who was Anne Frank?
She was a teenager who wrote...

1 ◯ a book about her life during the war.

2 ◯ a diary which was published after she died.

3 ◯ her autobiography.

2 **Have YOU ever read *Anne Frank: The Diary of a Young Girl*? If so, did you like it? If not, would you like to read it? Why?**

LISTENING

3 14 **Mark and Julia have to write an essay for school about *Anne Frank: The Diary of a Young Girl*. They have to hand in the essay tomorrow. Listen to their conversation and number the lines in the correct order.**

[5] *Mark* Come on. It's only the first draft. I'll get to school earlier tomorrow and write the final version before class.
[ ] *Julia* No, not yet. Have you?
[ ] *Julia* I would, but there's just one problem – I can't read your writing!
[ ] *Mark* Sure and I've written the essay too.
[1] *Mark* Have you finished reading *Anne Frank*?
[ ] *Julia* No kidding! You read much faster than me! Let me have a look. Oh, but your handwriting is awful!
[ ] *Mark* Hey, why don't you write up mine too?
[ ] *Julia* Yeah, and make sure you write more clearly if you want anybody to actually read it! I'm going to do mine on the computer.
[9] *Mark* That's not funny!

GO GET IT

comparative of adverbs

4 **Study the Language Login. Then fill in the chart with the comparative of the following adverbs.**

ADVERB	COMPARATIVE FORM
1 aggressively	more aggresively than
2 fast	faster than
3 fluently	___
4 quickly	___
5 well	___
6 hard	___

LANGUAGE LOGIN

Comparative of adverbs

Regular adverbs

clearly → Make sure you write **more clearly**.
carefully → My mom drives **more carefully than** my dad.

Irregular adverbs

early	→	I'll get to school	**earlier**	tomorrow.
fast	→	You read	**faster than**	me!
hard	→	My aunt works	**harder than**	my uncle!
well	→	Dan plays soccer	**better than**	Dilan.

PRACTICE

5 **Now use the comparative forms in #4 to make sentences comparing boys and girls. Use the prompts below.**

DIFFERENCES BETWEEN BOYS AND GIRLS

1 Girls / speak / fluently / boys.
Girls speak more fluently than boys.

2 Boys / behave / aggressively / girls.
___

3 Girls / learn new things / quickly / boys.
___

4 Boys / can run / fast / girls.
___

5 Boys / do / well / at / math / girls.
___

6 Girls / study / hard / boys.
___

Want more?
Go to Grammar Log – G3 (p. 90)

6 **Do YOU agree with the statements in #5?**

7 **In your notebook, write THREE sentences comparing YOURSELF to your best friend. You can use some of the topics below or choose others that interest you.**

do well at school or sports | dress well | run fast | talk loudly | study hard | get up early

Lesson 3

READING & COMPREHENSION

1 Read the blog and complete it using the words below.

accessory emos heads pants skaters

teen tribes

Tribes are groups of teens who have ideas and interests in common. Usually these teens become friends and make groups because they admire the same kind of music or like the same sport or style. Nowadays, there are many teen tribes in urban cities all over the world, such as the *trendies*, *nerds*, *indies*, [1] ________________ , *goths*, *punks* and *skaters*.

▶ my tribe

[2] ________________ belong to an almost exclusively boy tribe. It is very easy to identify skaters because their most characteristic [3] ________________ is a skateboard.

▶ what we wear

Skaters usually wear super large T-shirts and baggy [4] ________________ or long shorts. To complete the image they wear brand name sneakers and wear woollen berets or caps on their [5] ________________ .

2 Do YOU belong to any teen tribes? Which one?

3 Joey and Rita are friends and both are bloggers. Read their dialogue and write T for *true* and F for *false*.

15

Joey Hey, Rita. Have you read my blog lately?

Rita Yeah. I loved that article you posted about skaters. I even showed it to my dad.

Joey What did you do that for?

Rita Because Dad used to be a skater when he was young.

Joey Are you serious? Mr. Morgan? A skater?

Rita Unbelievable, isn't it? In the early 80's my dad used to ride ramps in New York and he was known as Crazy Eddie.

Joey That's awesome! So what did he look like then?

Rita Well, he's shown me some pictures. He used to have long hair and in the pictures he was always wearing shorts and a T-shirt.

Joey No way! I can only imagine him in a suit and tie.

Rita I know! But he, obviously, didn't use to wear a suit when he was fifteen. That's only because of his job!

Joey It is just hard to imagine your dad in skater's clothes. Do you think he would talk to me about his experience as a skater?

Rita Sure. I guess he would love to relive the good old days a bit!

1 [ ] Rita's father is a skater.
2 [ ] Rita's father's name is Mr. Morgan.
3 [ ] Mr. Morgan's nickname when he was young was Crazy Eddie.
4 [ ] Joey wants to ask Mr. Morgan to write an article for his blog.

GO GET IT

used to

4 **Study the Language Login. Look at Mr. Morgan's pictures in #3. Now complete the sentences about him with *used to* or *didn't use to*.**

In the 1980's Mr. Morgan...

1 ______________________ wear a suit.

2 ______________________ wear a cap.

5 **What did Rita say about her father? Circle the correct option.**

1 Dad **used to be / was** a skater when he was young.
2 Dad **rode / used to ride** ramps in New York.
3 He **used to have / had** long hair.
4 Dad **didn't wear / didn't use to wear** a suit when he was fifteen.

LANGUAGE LOGIN

Used to + infinitive (aff. & neg.)

Affirmative

Mr. Morgan He	**used to**	be a skater. ride ramps. have long hair.

Negative

Mr. Morgan He	**didn't use to**	wear formal clothes. work in an office. live in a small town.

Attention! We use **used to** and **didn't use to** to talk about past habits and states which are no longer true.

PRACTICE

6 **Look at the pictures of Mrs. Morgan, Rita's mom, and make sentences about what she *used to* do or *didn't use to* do in the 1980s.**

1 be a goth
She used to be a goth.

2 wear black clothes
____

3 dye her hair blond
____

4 wear lots of make up
____

5 smile a lot
____

6 have long hair
____

LOG IN

7 **Practice with a classmate.**
Talk about what YOU *used to* do or *didn't use to* do when you were a 10-year-old child. You can talk about the topics below.

What you used to do in your free time.	What TV programs you used to watch.
Who you used to play with.	What kind of clothes you used to wear.

A I used to play with dolls.
B Me too. / I didn't. I used to play video games.

Lesson 4

READING & COMPREHENSION

1 **Anna, a reporter for a teen website, interviewed her Grandma Beatrice about her teen years back in the 50's. Read the interview and check (✓) the topics they talk about.**

16

◯ school life ◯ housework
◯ free time ◯ her first job

Are we happier than the teens in Philadelphia in the 50's?

Being a teenager today is pretty hard. We have to deal with lots of things such as school, friends, family, and, of course, keeping up with the latest fashion. With all this in mind, I decided to interview my Grandma Beatrice to find out if teenagers in other generations had the same issues, dreams and hopes.

» **What did you use to do on weekends when you were a teenager, Grandma?**
First of all, you must remember we had Elvis Presley and the birth of rock and roll in the 50's. Saturdays were special days: we used to go to dances and watch the American Bandstand TV Show. We had a lot of fun dancing and chatting with the boys.

» **And how did your parents react to that?**
Oh, that was a problem. We used to have a record player in our living room and our parents decided what to play on it. We wanted to listen to rock and roll, but my mom and dad didn't like it. So we were forced to listen to our parents' music.

» **So, did you use to listen to rock and roll at all?**
We sure did! We used to go to the soda fountain after school and listen to Elvis's songs there. We didn't use to have our own CD player or MP3 player like you teens have today.

» **Did you use to spend a lot of money on clothes?**
No, we didn't. We used to make our own clothes, not buy them. All the girls knew how to sew and every home had a sewing machine.

» **Did you use to spend a long time helping your mom around the house?**
Yes, we did. I remember that my mother, your great-grandma, used to wash all our clothes by hand and when washing machines were invented she didn't want to use them. The same thing happened when Dad bought a vacuum cleaner.

» **Do you believe that teenagers in the 50's were happier than modern teens?**
Yes, I think so. Life was less complicated when I was young and we did not have the stresses of modern life. Anyway, I still believe that the teenage years are the best years of our lives no matter when they happen.

As we can see, despite technology and all the facilities modern life has to offer, Grandma honestly feels that her generation was happier. Personally, I think she might be right.

Anna

2 **Read the interview in #1 again and write T for *true* and F for *false*.**

1 [ ] Beatrice enjoyed going to dances.
2 [ ] Beatrice used to buy lots of new clothes when she was young.
3 [ ] Beatrice thinks being a teen today is better than in the 50's.

VOCABULARY WORK

household appliances

3 **Find the THREE missing words for these household appliances in the interview in #1.**

1 dishwasher

2 microwave oven

3 ______

4 ______

5 stove

6 ______

LANGUAGE LOGIN

Used to + infinitive (int.)

Interrogative

				Short answers
Did	you	**use to**	spend a lot of money on clothes?	**Yes**, we **did**.
	they		sew their own clothes?	**Yes**, they **did**.
	Grandma		have lots of household appliances?	**No**, she **didn't**.
	the teens		have their own record players?	**No**, they **didn't**.

What **did** you **use to** do on weekends? / wear?

We **used to** go to dances. / wear dresses I made myself.

GO GET IT

used to (int.)

4 Study the Language Login and:

1 check (✓) the correct option below.
The interrogative form of *used to* ◯ **is** ◯ **isn't** the same for all persons.

2 underline TWO other examples of the interrogative form of *used to* in Anna's blog in #1.

7
air conditioner

8
fridge

9
radio

PRACTICE

5 Anna became curious about her mom's childhood and decided to ask her some questions. Use the prompts to write the questions Anna asked.

1 (cry a lot)
Did you use to cry a lot?
Not really. I think I was a pretty happy kid.

2 (fight with Aunt Julie)
____
Oh yes. My sister and I had huge fights when we were kids.

3 (your parents / let you go out)
____
Mom was stricter than Dad, but they used to let me go out. Most of the times, that is.

4 (dream of having a daughter)
____
Absolutely. That was my biggest dream, and I am so glad it came true!

LOG IN

6 Writing.
Imagine it is the year 2050. Your grandson or granddaughter has asked you to write about your teenage years. In your notebook, write a short paragraph about your life today. You can write about the topics below.

Family and friends / Activities you do in your free time / School / Your interests (sports, music etc.) / Clothes

Example: *When I was a teenager back at the beginning of the century, I used to live in a small apartment with my family. My best friends at the time were... We used to do everything together. We used to...*

Want more?
Go to Grammar Log – G4 (p. 91)

1 **Do the crosswords puzzle and complete the sentences with suitable adverbs. The first letter of each adverb has been given to you.**

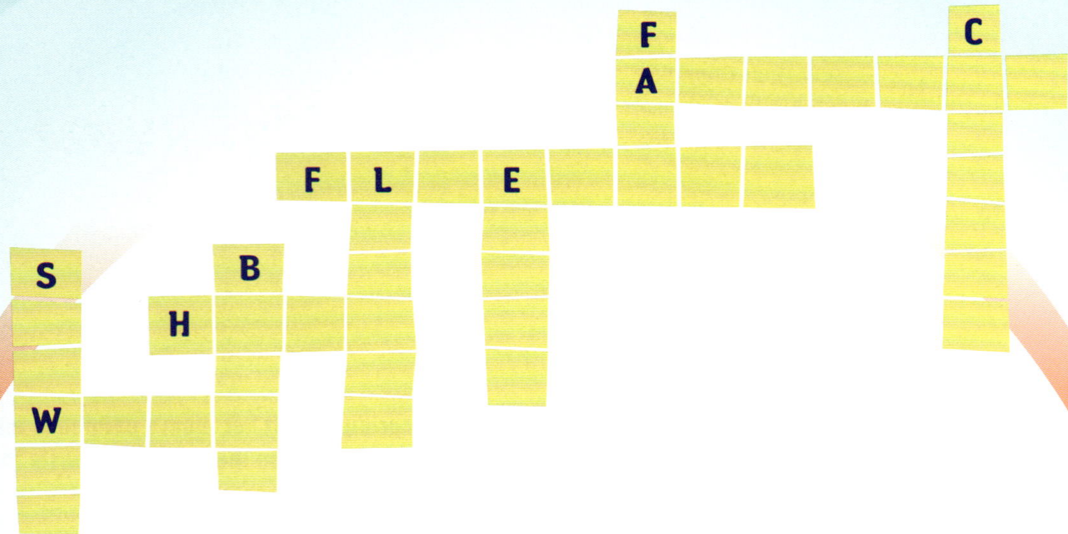

ACROSS

1 My dad has never had a car accident. He drives very w______________ .
2 I'm going to study h______________ for that test!
3 You must practice if you want to speak German f______________ .
4 "Be quiet!" Josh said a______________ to his brother.

DOWN

1 Hurry up! You walk too s______________ !
2 His team lost the game because they played very b______________ .
3 Shh! Don't speak so l______________ ! We're in a hospital!
4 Why did you arrive so e______________ ?
5 Winona can't run very f______________ .
6 I can't understand him. He doesn't speak very c______________ .

2 **Make sentences using adverbs from #1 in the comparative form. Follow the example.**

1 She studies hard. Her sister doesn't study so hard. *She studies harder than her sister.*
2 They arrived really early and the teacher arrived later. *They* ______________
3 She can dance very well, but her friends dance very badly. ______________
4 You speak loud. The other students don't speak so loud. ______________
5 Sam writes clearly. Paula doesn't write very clearly. ______________
6 My mom drives fast. My sister doesn't drive so fast. ______________

3 **Think about FOUR people YOU admire. Write sentences comparing them to other people. Use adverbs. Follow the example.**

Felipe Massa drives faster than Rubens Barrichello.

4 **Look at the pictures. Then complete the questions and give the answers.**

1 __Did__ Gabriella __use to have__ short hair? __Yes, she did.__.
2 ______ Angela ______ in a house? ______.
3 ______ Angela ______ glasses? ______.
4 ______ Angela ______ braces? ______.
5 ______ Justin and Jordan ______ play together? ______.

5 **Read the information about Haru, a young Japanese who creates incredible manga stories. Look at the table below and finish the paragraph about Haru's past and present.**

	HARU – 7 YEARS OLD	HARU – NOW (22 YEARS OLD)
Place of residence	Japan	Brazil
Language(s)	Japanese only	Japanese, Portuguese and English
Favorite activity	drawing	drawing and playing the guitar
Occupation	student	manga designer and writer
Personality	shy and quiet	sociable and funny
Dreams	being a great Pokémon trainer	having his own company

When Haru was 7 years old he used to live in Japan. Now he lives in Brazil. He used to speak only one language, Japanese, but now he ______

______

______

______

Want more?
Go to Word Log U3 (p. 98)

Unit 4

Make up your mind

Lesson 1

READING & COMPREHENSION

1 **With the help of your teacher and / or a dictionary, match the words and pictures. Write A-F next to the words.**

A

B

C

D

E

F

1 [ ] farmers
2 [ ] a slum
3 [ ] seeds
4 [ ] oil
5 [ ] cosmetic industry
6 [ ] fishermen

2 **The words in #1 appear in the text in #3. What do YOU think the text might be about?**

3 17 **Read the article and check your predictions. Find out what *World Challenge* is and check (✓) the correct options in the sentences.**

What is World Challenge?

World Challenge is a global competition and its objective is to find projects or small businesses that have shown innovation and made a difference to the local community. Since it began in January 2004 *World Challenge* has received lots of nominations from all over the world. These include, for example, projects that have helped farmers in Peru or improved the lives of people in the slums of Colombia. Each year thousands of people vote to say who they think deserves to win. One of the 2007 nominees was from a rural community in the Brazilian Amazon. Marajo Island is the largest fresh water island in the world, and for years the 200,000 people who live there have worked in the fishing industry during the dry season, when the river is full of fish. But during the rainy season the fish disappear. That is also the time when the Andiroba trees deposit their seeds. These seeds are carried by the rivers and many end up on the beaches of Marajo. For years the fishermen from Marajo have considered these seeds a problem but a Brazilian company saw an opportunity to make money out of them. In 2004, this company organized a cooperative to collect the seeds and extract their oil for the cosmetics industry. Life on the island has improved for many families since 2004. This project has made a huge difference for the families of the 1,000 people working in the business.

If you want to know more about *World Challenge* and the nominated projects, visit: www.theworldchallenge.co.uk

1 *World Challenge* is a
◯ **charity** ◯ **competition** ◯ **race**.

2 Nominations come from all over
◯ **Asia** ◯ **Latin America** ◯ **the world**.

LANGUAGE LOGIN

Present perfect with *for* & *since*

for

The islanders **have worked** in the fishing industry **for** years.
World Challenge **has existed for** more than five years.
João **has worked** on the project **for** three years.

since

Life **has improved** for many families on the island **since** 2004.
They **have collected** thousands of tones of seeds **since** the project started.
João **has lived** on this island **since** he was born.

Attention! Use ________ + a fixed point of time in the past.
Use ________ + a period of time up to the present.

4 **Complete the sentences with the correct numbers according to the article.**

1 *World Challenge* has existed for more than ________________ years.
2 Marajo Island has a population of approximately ________________ people.
3 About ________________ islanders are employed in the business.
4 Life on the island of Marajo has improved since ________________.

GOT GET IT

present perfect + for & since

5 **Read the Language Login and then complete the rules with *for* or *since*.**

PRACTICE

6 **Circle the correct option.**

1 I have known John **for / since** a long time.
2 My dad has worked in this company **for / since** 1999.
3 He hasn't seen his family **for / since** last year.
4 My boyfriend hasn't called me **for / since** two days.
5 I haven't failed a test **for / since** years.

7 **Complete the sentences with information about YOU and your family. Use the *Present perfect* tense.**

1 I ________________ (study) at my present school for ________________.
2 I ________________ (live) in my present home since ________________.
3 My parents ________________ (know) each other for ________________.
4 My father / mother ________________ (work) as a ________________ since ________________.

LOG IN

8 **Practice with a classmate.**
Make guesses about YOUR classmates. Use the prompts and/or your own ideas.

have those shoes / jeans
have that watch / cell phone — have long / short hair
study English — have lived in (city) — know the teacher

Example:
A Pedro has had those jeans for three years. Is that right, Pedro?
B No, sorry. I've had these jeans for six months. My turn now. Alice has lived in this city since last year. Is that right, Alice?
C That's right. Well done! My turn now.

VOCABULARY WORK

occupations

1 **Read the names of the different places below and then say who might work there. Write different occupations.**

1 In a hospital: doctors, surgeons, nurses, cleaners, cooks, nutritionists

2 On a building site: ______

3 On a farm: ______

4 On a boat: ______

5 In an office building: ______

Lesson 2

LISTENING & COMPREHENSION

2 **Chloe Walters has a very unusual occupation. She is a shark keeper. Listen to a podcast interview and put a cross (✗) next to the task which she doesn't mention as part of her job.**

18

- ◯ clean the aquarium
- ◯ organize the aquarium exhibits
- ◯ do research on the sharks
- ◯ talk to the visitors
- ◯ feed the sharks

3 **Listen to the interview again and check (✓) what you hear.**

1 **Interviewer** How long ◯ have you worked as a shark keeper? ◯ do you work as a shark keeper?

2 **Interviewer** How long ◯ are you a professional diver? ◯ have you been a professional diver?

LANGUAGE LOGIN

How long + Present perfect

How long ________ you ________ as a shark keeper?	For two years.
________ *have* you *been* a professional diver?	For two years.
How long *has* Chloe *worked* at that aquarium?	Since she left college.
How long *have* the sharks *been* there?	For a year or so.

Attention! When asking questions with *how long*, we use the verb in the **Present perfect / Present simple** tense.

GO GET IT

how long + present perfect

4 **Read the questions in #3 again and complete the Language Login questions. Then circle the correct option to complete the rule.**

PRACTICE

5 **Use the prompts to make questions using the *Present perfect*. Then write YOUR answers to the questions**

1 you / study English
Q How long have you studied English?
A ________

2 you / had your cell phone
Q ________
____
A ________

3 your family / live in your present home
Q ________
____
A ________

4 you / be at school today
Q ________
____
A ________

LOG IN

6 **Practice with a classmate.**
Together with a classmate, think of a professional YOU both know and can talk to at school. Try to answer the questions. Guess the answers you don't know. Then, interview the person chosen and check who got closer to the real facts: you or your classmate?

1 What does he / she do?
____

2 Where does he / she work?
____

3 How long has he / she done this job?
____

4 Why did he / she decide to do this job?
____

5 What does he / she think of this job?
____

Want more?
Go to Grammar Log – G5 (p. 91)

READING & COMPREHENSION

1 Read the results of a survey that took place in the USA. Then answer the questions.

1 Do you think the results would be similar if the same survey was done in **YOUR** country?

2 What do you think the TOP THREE career choices for teens in your country are?

1 ______________________________

2 ______________________________

3 ______________________________

TEEN'S TOP 10 CAREER CHOICES

We asked teens to pick three occupations they would like to have in the future.
Here are the most popular choices:

1 teacher
2 doctor
3 lawyer
4 athlete
5 scientist / biologist
6 architect
7 businessperson
8 engineer
9 IT consultant
10 nurse

Lesson 3

2 Read what three young Americans said in the interview for the survey above. Write the occupations they would like to have under their names.

19

My parents work in the business world and I can see they have pretty stressful lives. They always seem to be worried about things and never seem to relax, so I know that I definitely don't want to be a businessman! [4] My dream is to play baseball for the New York Yankees in Yankee stadium. It must be so exciting! [ ] And athletes are well-paid too!

1

Dennis

____

2

Kelly

____

I'd really like to be a doctor – it must be really rewarding, especially when you save people's lives. But I don't think I am going to get good enough grades to study medicine. [ ] The exams for nursing are not as difficult as the exams for medicine and I think the job is really interesting. My aunt is a nurse and she tells me it can be very tiring as you often have to work night shifts. [ ]

I don't really know yet what I want to do. I know I definitely don't want to work in an office on a computer all day – that must be really boring. I'd probably fall asleep! [ ] I want a job which involves working with people. [ ] I'm good at entertaining small kids and they always love me, so that's why I'd like to be an elementary school teacher. I know it can be badly-paid, that it isn't as well-paid as other jobs, but money isn't everything!

3

Mia

____

3 The sentences below were taken from the texts in #2. Read the interviews again and place them in the right spot.

1 That's why I think nursing will probably be better for me.
2 So an office job is out for me!
3 Just imagine being there with all the fans cheering and shouting!
4 They hope that I will become a lawyer, but I really want to be a baseball player.
5 But she also says it is so good when you see how you can really make a difference in people's lives.
6 I guess teaching could be fun.

VOCABULARY WORK

adjectives for describing jobs

4 Use the highlighted adjectives in #2 to complete the sentences.

1 A ______________ job will cause you a lot of worry.
2 A ______________ job might make you fall asleep.
3 If you have an ______________ job you get involved and want to learn more.
4 An ______________ job makes you happy and enthusiastic.
5 A ______________ job leaves you exhausted.
6 A ______________ job gives you a lot of personal satisfaction.
7 If you're ______________ you don't have a good salary.
8 A ______________ job gives you a good salary.

LANGUAGE LOGIN

Not as... as

The nursing exams are **not as** difficult **as** the exams for medicine.	→	The nursing exams are **easier** / **more difficult** than the exams for medicine.
Teaching is **not as** well-paid **as** many other jobs.	→	Teaching is **better** / **worse** paid than many other jobs. Other jobs are better-paid.

GO GET IT

not as... as

5 **Read the Language Login and circle the correct option to explain the meaning of the example sentences.**

PRACTICE

6 **Use the prompts to make sentences using *not as... as*. Follow the model.**

1 Being a teacher / stressful / being a doctor
Being a teacher isn't as stressful as being a doctor.

2 working in an office / exciting / working in a summer camp

____

____

3 architects / well-paid / engineers

____

____

4 working for a big company / rewarding / doing voluntary work

____

____

5 teaching adults / tiring / teaching teenagers

____

____

7 **What is YOUR opinion? Do you agree or disagree with the sentences in #6?**

8 **Now compare the items below. Choose the adjectives you want to use and give YOUR opinion. Look at the example.**

1 famous soccer players – famous gymnasts
Famous soccer players are better-paid than famous gymnasts.
Famous gymnasts are not as well-paid as famous soccer players.

2 playing indoors – playing outdoors

____

3 speaking Spanish – speaking English

____

4 team work – individual work

____

9 **Play a game: *guess my job*. Think of an occupation. Answer *yes* or *no* to your classmates' questions to help them find out what occupation you thought of.**

Examples:

Guess my job

A Is it a well-paid job?
You Yes, it is.
B Do you work in an office?
You No, I don't.
C Do you need to wear a uniform?
You Yes, I do.
D Can it be a stressful job?
You Yes, it can.
A Do you work outdoors?
You Yes, I do.
B Do people watch you work?
You Yes, they do.
C I know! You are an athlete!
You That's right. / No! You lose.

Want more?
Go to Grammar Log – G6 (p. 92)

READING & COMPREHENSION

1 **Read these different jobs and check (✓) the ones that YOU think will be in demand in twenty years' time and put a cross (✗) next to the jobs that probably won't exist anymore.**

1 ◯ a CD store manager
2 ◯ a fighter pilot
3 ◯ a hairdresser
4 ◯ a politician
5 ◯ a robot mechanic
6 ◯ a space tour guide
7 ◯ a video shop assistant

2 **Quickly read this online article from a site for teens and check (✓) the best title.**

20

◯ New jobs in the 21st century. ◯ Making choices about your future. ◯ Technology changes professions.

Lesson 4

Young people thinking about their future should think carefully about any career choices they make. Some jobs may not exist in twenty years' time. For example, don't consider being a CD store manager. Who's going to go to your store when they can search for music online? Here are a few new jobs for you to consider, professions that we are sure people will need in twenty years' time:

A SPACE TOUR GUIDE

Pleasure trips to space are not so far away. *Virgin Galactic* will soon offer trips to space for about $200,000. So if you are interested in going to space and don't have $200,000 to spend, perhaps you should contact *Virgin Galactic* and check the qualifications needed for a space tour guide!

A FLOODED CITY SPECIALIST

If climate change happens more quickly than expected, who is going to be responsible for all the flood victims? According to some futurists, there will be a lot of new jobs around flooded cities: specialized divers will be needed to rescue people and objects. Because houses will need to be moved to higher ground, architects and engineers with special qualifications will have a lot of work to do.

A ROBOT MECHANIC

There are cleaners and gardeners worried about losing their jobs as robots start to take over. Many robots in the market can clean carpets, filter pools or mow lawns. In a few years, these machines will be cheaper and everyone will be able to buy robotic personal assistants or companions (robotic pets). All these machines will need occasional tune-up, so if you are good at repairing things, perhaps you should consider a career as a robot mechanic.

3 **Answer the questions according to the article in #2.**

1 Is *Virgin Galactic* already offering trips to space?

____

2 If climate change happens more quickly than expected, what will probably happen?

____

3 What will specialized divers do?

____

4 Why are there cleaners and gardeners worried about losing their jobs?

____

5 Why might working as a robot mechanic be a good career in the future?

____

____

GO GET IT

adjective + prepositions + noun /- ing

4 **Use the highlighted expressions in #2 to complete the sentences in the Language Login.**

LANGUAGE LOGIN

Adjective + prepositions + noun / -ing

When I was a child I was **fascinated by** dinosaurs.

A film director is **responsible** ________________ the final product you see on screen.

I'm ________________ **in** learning about other cultures.

Many people today are ________________ losing their jobs.

My sister is really ________________ painting.

I am really **bad at** math.

He's **afraid of** heights so he could never be a fireman.

PRACTICE

5 **Match the sentence halves.**

1 I have always been fascinated
2 I'm really afraid
3 If I get the job, I'll be responsible
4 I'm very interested
5 My brother is very good
6 My mom is really bad
7 I am very worried

[ ] of flying so I could never be a flight attendant.
[ ] about our planet and its future.
[ ] at computer programming. He wants to be a game designer.
[ ] for clients in Latin America.
[1] by planets and space, so I'd love to be a space tour guide.
[ ] in languages, so I'd like to travel abroad.
[ ] at remembering people's names, which isn't good for a teacher!

6 **Read this introduction to a forum discussion. Then read the posting and circle the correct options to complete it.**

WHAT JOB DO YOU WANT WHEN YOU'RE OLDER?

Many teens in the USA say working with computers would be their ideal job, even more than being a pop star. I.T. is a firm favorite with teens because of good money and exciting technology. But what is your dream job? Is a computer-related job your ideal occupation? Are you looking for a big salary, or do you want a job you can enjoy? Or both?

posted: Sat 16 10 p.m. Post subject: What job do you want when you're older?

citykid

When I am older I'd like to work as [1] **a / an / Ø** architect. I've been interested [2] **for / in / of** buildings and design [3] **for / how long / since** I was about five. I've always been really good [4] **at / for / to** art and when I was small I [5] **usually / use / used** to draw pictures of buildings and houses all the time, so my parents weren't surprised by my choice. I know the salary isn't as good [6] **as / than / of** a computing job, but for me doing something I enjoy is much [7] **as / more / less** important than money. I think it must be so [8] **tiring / rewarding / stressful** to see something you have designed become real.

LOG IN

7 **Writing.**
In your notebook, write YOUR answer to the forum questions in the form of a paragraph. Use the text in #6 as a model. Include at least two examples of an adjective + preposition and one example of *not as + as*.
When I am older I'd like to...

Want more?
Go to Grammar Log – G7 (p. 92)

1 **Read about Ben Stiller, a famous American actor. Choose the correct option (a, b or c) to complete the article.**

Benjamin Stiller [1] ___was___ born on October 30, 1965, in New York City. He [2] __________ in contact with the artistic world since very young as both his parents were comedy actors.

Ben [3] __________ interested in movies since early age so after graduating from high school in 1983, he [4] __________ film studies at UCLA (University of California – Los Angeles) but [5] __________ after nine months and went back to New York.

He [6] __________ various films and TV shows, including many comedies, Ben's special talent. He [7] __________ some experience as a director too, something Ben really enjoys doing.

He [8] __________ his first experience as a director in *Reality Bites* in 1994, and since then he [9] __________, starred in, directed, and produced over fifty films and television shows.

Ben [10] __________ his way to fame with his special and unique kind of humor. He [11] __________ one of the most wanted comics in the business.

Based on www.westlord.com/benstiller (accessed August 2008)

	a	b	c
1	(a) was	b has been	c have been
2	a has been	b was	c have been
3	a was	b have been	c has been
4	a started	b has started	c have started
5	a have given up	b has given up	c gave up
6	a has taken part in	b took part in	c taken part in
7	a had	b have had	c has had
8	a have had	b had	c has had
9	a has written	b have written	c wrote
10	a fought	b has fought	c have fought
11	a has become	b became	c have become

2 **Read the text again and answer the questions about Ben Stiller.**

1 How long has Ben been involved with the artistic world?

____

2 How old was he when he graduated from high school?

____

3 According to the article, what is Ben's special talent?

____

____

3 **This is Mia. Make questions about her using *how long*.**

1 Mia is Ben's fan.
How long has Mia been Ben's fan?

2 Mia lives in LA.

____

3 Mia knows Tania.

____

4 Noah, Mia's boyfriend, is sick.

____

5 Mia and Tania study at UCLA.

____

Review

4 **Look at the pictures and complete the answers to the questions in #3. Use *for* or *since*.**

1 ____________ three years.

2 ____________ two years.

3 ____________ elementary school.

4 ____________ last Tuesday.

5 ____________ the beginning of the year.

5 **Complete the sentences with a suitable adjective.**

1 Taking lots of tests can be really ___stressful___ .

2 You might fall asleep while in a ____________________ class.

3 When we have a good teacher, the subject we have to study becomes more ____________________ .

4 An ____________________ subject will make you feel enthusiastic and ready to learn more.

5 My mom is a teacher. She thinks that teaching is a tiring job, but very ____________________ , as it gives her a lot of personal satisfaction.

6 **Think about someone YOU know very well. What do you know about him or her? Use the expressions in the box and write sentences using *(not) as... as*.**

responsible for	afraid of	fascinated by	interested in	bad at	good at	worried about

Example: My sister is not as afraid of dogs as my brother.

____

____

____

Want more?
Go to Word Log U4 (p. 99)

Unit 5

My mind is made up

Lesson 1

READING & COMPREHENSION

1 **Read the texts below and write the names of the people they refer to.**

David Beckham · Lars Grael · Jô Soares · Regina Casé · Lucy Liu

1 ___Jô Soares___ is a Brazilian comedian, presenter and writer. He wrote a great book called *Xangô de Baker Street*. He is very clever and witty.

2 ______________ is American but her parents are Chinese. She was a shy girl but she grew up to be a beautiful, extroverted actress. She is short and slim and I think she is really cool.

3 ______________ is a Brazilian yachtsman. He is very determined. He had a serious accident in 1998 and lost a leg. But, he went back sailing a couple of months later. He is my idol!

4 ______________ is a Brazilian comedian, actress and presenter. She is chubby and very funny. She seems to be an easy-going and kind person.

5 ______________ is a famous British soccer player. He is athletic and blond. He is generous too. He usually takes part in charity events. He is absolutely gorgeous!

2 **Do YOU know the people in #1? What do you think of them?**

VOCABULARY WORK

adjectives for describing people

3 **Look at the highlighted adjectives in #1. In your notebook categorize them: *appearance* or *personality*.**

APPEARANCE	PERSONALITY
beautiful	clever

Now try to add other adjectives you can use to describe a person's appearance and personality to your lists.

LANGUAGE LOGIN

What + look like? vs. What + be + like?

What does Lucy Liu **look like**?	She's short and slim.
What do you **look like**?	I have brown hair and blue eyes.
What do they **look like**?	They are blond and gorgeous.
What is Beckham **like**?	He's athletic and generous.
What are you **like**?	I'm serious and determined.
What is your city **like**?	It's big and clean.

Attention! 1 *What + look like* is a question about ____________.

2 *What + be + like* is a question about ____________ and / or ____________.

LISTENING & COMPREHENSION

4 21 **Kate and Pat are best friends. Listen to their phone conversation about a new boy in town. Check (✓) the picture of the boy they are describing.**

5 22 **Listen to two extracts from the conversation in #5 and circle the correct alternative.**

1 *Kate* **What does he look like? / What is he like?**
Pat Oh, he's gorgeous! He's tall and athletic. He has brown hair and blue eyes, and a beautiful smile!

2 *Kate* Wow! And **what does he look like? / what's he like?**
Pat Well, we talked for about an hour. He's very intelligent and witty. He has a sharp sense of humor. And he's very kind too.

GO GET IT

look like & be like

6 **Look at the Language Login and complete the rules with *personality* or *appearance*.**

PRACTICE

7 **Complete the questions and then match them to the corresponding answers.**

1 What does Johnny look like ?
2 ____________ his hair like?
3 ____________ your grandparents ____________ ?
4 What does your girlfriend ____________ ?
5 ____________ your dog ____________ ?

[ ] It's short and curly.
[1] He is athletic and he has a tattoo on his arm.
[ ] She's blond and very good-looking.
[ ] He's big, furry and very friendly.
[ ] They're kind and funny.

LOG IN

8 **Practice with a classmate.**
Ask questions about your classmate's family, friends and life. Then answer about YOU.
Talk about: parents' appearance, neighborhood, best friend's personality, bedroom, pets etc.

Example:
A What does your father look like?
B He's very tall. He has brown eyes and...

Want more?
Go to Grammar Log – G8 (p. 92)

READING & COMPREHENSION

1 **Look at the pictures. What do these people have in common?**

____

2 **What do YOU know about tattoos? What would you like to know? In your notebook, write down some questions you would like to ask about tattoos.**

3 **Read these *Frequently Asked Questions* (FAQ) about tattoos. Can you find the answers to any of YOUR questions?**

23

TATTO(FAQ)

1 What is a tattoo?
A tattoo is a permanent picture or message on the skin which is created with a needle and ink.

2 How long have tattoos been around?
Believe it or not, tattoos have been used as body adornment by many cultures for over 5,000 years.

3 How old do I have to be to get a tattoo?
Usually 18. But this can vary from country to country.

4 What sort of equipment is used?
A tattoo machine, which is an electric instrument that uses a needle system to mark the skin with ink.

5 Does it hurt to get a tattoo?
Actually, getting a tattoo is not very painful nowadays because modern tattoo equipment is so good that the needles go in and out of your skin very quickly (about 80 to 150 times per second). But, of course, the level of discomfort will depend on the design of the tattoo and its location.

6 Is it safe to get a tattoo?
If you go to a tattoo shop that uses the proper tattoo equipment and has the necessary safety policies (for example, throwing away the needles after using them) then you don't run the risk of getting hepatitis C or any other contagious diseases.

4 **Check (✓) the correct statements according to the FAQ above. Correct the wrong ones.**

1 ◯ Tattooing is an ancient art. ______________________________
2 ◯ You have to be eighteen to get a tattoo. ______________________________
3 ◯ Getting a tattoo is completely painless. ______________________________
4 ◯ To have a safe tattoo you must go to a professional tattoo shop. ______________________________

LANGUAGE LOGIN

Relative clauses with *who, which* & *that*

A tattoo is a permanent picture on the skin.
A tattoo is created with a needle and ink.

↓

A tattoo is a permanent picture on the skin **which / that** is created with a needle and ink.

A tattoo artist is an artist. **A tattoo artist** has a lot of responsibility because the art he creates is permanent.

↓

A tattoo artist is an artist **who / that** has a lot of responsibility because the art he creates is permanent.

GO GET IT

relative clauses with who, which & that

5 Study the Language Login and complete the rules below with *who* or *which*.

1 When the sentence refers to *people*, we use ______________ or *that*.

2 When the sentence refers to *things*, we use ______________ or *that*.

6 Find examples of relative clauses in the FAQ texts in #3 and underline them.

PRACTICE

7 Complete the sentences with *who* or *which*.

1 A tattoo machine is a machine __________ injects ink into your skin with a needle.

2 An apprentice is a person __________ is learning to become a tattoo artist.

3 *Miami Ink* is a famous TV show __________ presents the life and work of some American tattoo artists.

4 Ami James and Chris Nuñez are famous tattoo artists __________ appear on a TV show.

5 Fairies, crosses and tribal designs are the tattoos __________ are the most popular in the USA.

8 Join the sentences using the relative pronouns *who*, *which* or *that*.

1 Kat Von D is a female tattoo artist. She works in Los Angeles.
Kat von D is a female tattoo artist who / that works in Los Angeles.

2 English is a language. It is spoken all over the world.
____
____

3 A helmet is an object. It protects the head.
____
____

4 Chris Nuñez is a tattoo artist. He lived in Brazil for five years.
____
____

LOG IN

9 Practice with a classmate.
In a piece of paper write the name of an animal, an occupation and an object. Then give your classmate THREE clues and THREE chances to guess what it is. Follow the model.

Example:
A It's a person who is very well-paid.
B A businessperson!
A No, it isn't. It's a person who works on a team.
B A soccer player?
A No, it isn't. It's a person who plays a popular sport in the USA.
B A baseball player?
A That's right. Well done!

READING & COMPREHENSION

1 **Read this online magazine page called *Teen Line* and complete the chart with information about it. Would YOU like to publish your work on *Teen Line*? Do you like reading magazines? Which are your favorite sections?**

24

Teen Line

Written by Teens.

About Us

Welcome to **Teen Line**, a bi-monthly magazine that offers teenagers the opportunity to speak for themselves. **Teen Line** is the place where teenagers can publish their creative work and opinions on the issues that affect their lives – everything from love and family to fashion and music. Thousands of students have submitted their work to us and we have published the work of more than 23,000 teens since 1995. Find out what other teens around the world are thinking, writing and creating. Then send us your work and let your voice be heard!

Poetry	Art gallery	Movie reviews	Book reviews	Sports	Music reviews
Heroes (NEW)	Beauty	Travel	Culture	Health	Interviews

Submit contributions to our new section. HEROES is the section where you can write about people you admire.

ABOUT THE ONLINE MAGAZINE

Magazine Title: [1] Teen Line

Written by: [2] ________

New issues: every [3] ________ months

Number of teens published: [4] ________

Number of different features: [5] ________

VOCABULARY WORK

magazine sections

2 **Look at the words in the blue boxes in #1 and find the section where teenagers...**

1 give their opinion of movies.
Movie reviews

2 write about different cultures and places.
____

3 write about people they admire.
____

4 show their paintings and pictures.
____

5 write about diets, hair styles, clothes etc.
____

6 publish their poems.
____

3 **Would YOU like to publish your work on *Teen Line*? Do you like reading magazines? Which are your favorite sections?**

GO GET IT

relative clauses with where

4 **Read the sentences in the Language Login on page 53 and circle the correct option to complete the rule.**

Lesson 3

LANGUAGE LOGIN

Relative clauses with *where*

Teen Line is the place		teenagers can publish their creative work.
Heroes is the section	**where**	teenagers can write about people they admire.
A school is a place		people study.

Attention! When the sentence refers to a **person / place** we use **where**.

PRACTICE

5 Match the columns and make sentences.

1 Second Life	is a virtual place where	[ ] you express your thoughts and experiences.
2 A wiki		[ ] people can "meet" online and have a conversation.
3 A blog		[1] people can take on a new identity called an *avatar*.
4 A chat room		[ ] all sorts of information can be stored and shared.

6 Make sentences using the prompts below. Follow the model.

1 supermarket / place / buy food — A supermarket is a place where you buy food.
2 library / place / borrow books ____________
3 arcade / place / play pinball and electronic games ____________
4 stadium / place / watch sports competitions ____________
5 airport / place / take a flight ____________

LOG IN

7 Practice with a classmate.
On a piece of paper write the places below in jumbled order to give information about YOU. After that, exchange pieces of paper and try to guess information about your classmate.

1 the place where you were born
2 the place where you spent your last vacation
3 a place where you would like to live
4 the street where you live
5 a street you used to live

Example:
A São Paulo. This is the place where you would like to live.
B No, that's wrong.
A So it's the place where you were born.
B Yes, that's right.

Want more? Go to Grammar Log – G9 (p. 93)

VOCABULARY WORK

clothes & physical appearance

1 **Look at the picture. What can YOU see?**

____
____
____
____
____
____

Lesson 4

2 **Now write the correct names. Who in the picture...**

1 is wearing baggy jeans? Paul ______
2 is wearing tight jeans? ______
3 has a tattoo? ______
4 has dyed hair? ______
5 is wearing designer clothes? ______
6 is wearing scruffy clothes? ______

LISTENING & COMPREHENSION

3 **Delia is showing the picture to a friend. Listen and read the dialogue and check (✓) what you hear.**

25

Delia Check it out, Olivia. This is my guitar teacher, Paul.
Olivia Which one?
Delia The one with the long hair in a ponytail.
Olivia He looks cool but a bit ◯ **scruffy** ◯ **nervous**.
Delia I know. He doesn't care about appearances.
Olivia And who is that girl?
Delia Which [1] one? The [2] one with a tattoo?
Olivia No. The one with the body piercing.
Delia Oh, that's Tereza, Paul's ◯ **sister** ◯ **wife**.
Olivia And who is the one with a tattoo?
Delia That's Makayla. She's a great ◯ **person** ◯ **singer**.
Olivia Oh, look at those shoes!
Delia Which [3] ones?
Olivia The [4] ones Makayla is ◯ **using** ◯ **wearing**. Awesome!
Delia I knew you would like them. Did you see my new guitar?
Olivia Which [5] one is it? The one you are playing?
Delia No. That's Chung-Ho's. Mine is the ◯ **brown** ◯ **black** one.
Olivia Chung-Ho, hum? I think I'll have to join your guitar lessons...

4 **Now answer the questions according to #3.**

1 In Delia's opinion, why is Paul scruffy?

____

2 Why did Olivia mention Makayla's shoes?

____

3 Do **YOU** think Olivia is interested in learning how to play the guitar?

____

LANGUAGE LOGIN

Pronouns: one / ones

Did you see my new guitar? Which **one** is it?
Look at those shoes! Which **ones**?

Attention! We use __________ to replace singular nouns and __________ to replace plural nouns.

5 **Look at the highlighted words in #3 and check (✓) what each word refers to.**

1 ◯ girl ◯ girls
2 ◯ girls ◯ girl
3 ◯ tattoos ◯ shoes
4 ◯ shoes ◯ girls
5 ◯ guitar ◯ girl

GO GET IT

one & ones

6 **Now study the examples in the Language Login and complete the rule with *one* or *ones*.**

PRACTICE

7 **Complete the dialogues with *one* or *ones*.**

1 A I've just bought Tricia a nice present for her birthday.
B Oh, I completely forgot about it. I have to buy her __________ too.

2 A Would you like a glass of soda?
B No, thanks. I've just had __________ .

3 A Which CDs would you like me to take?
B The __________ next to the TV.

4 A Can you lend me a pen?
B Sorry, I don't have __________ .

5 A Which sneakers do you prefer: the red __________ or the white __________ ?
B I think the read __________ are cool.

READING & COMPREHENSION

8 **Delia likes writing and publishing her creative work on *Teen Line Magazine*. She wrote about her guitar teacher for the HERO section. Read her description of Paul and match the paragraphs and their topics.**

Teen Line
Written by Teens.

PAUL

By Delia Kane, Connecticut

[1] When I decided to write an essay on a modern-day hero who has been important in my life, I immediately thought about my guitar teacher Paul. Paul is 30 years old and he is the one who has taught me that music can change our mind and spirit.

[2] Paul is short and a bit chubby. He has brown eyes and long hair which he usually wears in a ponytail. He doesn't care much about clothes, so he usually wears scruffy T-shirts and old baggy jeans.

[3] Paul is a very generous person who thinks that pleasure is more important than money. He always invites people to play at his house and is never too tired to teach new songs. He is a very relaxed person who practices yoga and eats healthy food. Every Sunday morning he plays for the children at the local hospital. It's amazing to see how happy they get when Paul arrives.

[4] I met Paul two years ago and now I know that music can bring a lot of peace to our lives. Paul and my guitar are now my best friends.

1 Personality [ ] Paragraph 1
2 Introducing the hero [4] Paragraph 2
3 Conclusion [ ] Paragraph 3
4 Physical appearance [ ] Paragraph 4

LOG IN

9 **Writing.**
In your notebook, write a description of a hero for *Teen Line*. Use the text in #8 as a model.

Want more?
Go to Grammar Log – G10 (p. 93)

1 **Complete the blog post below using words from the box. There are extra words which will NOT be used.**

one	wear	which	wearing	where	ones	who	outgoing

There are lots of different tribes of teenagers, with different thoughts and styles. [1] ________________ of them is called Emo. Emos are usually sensitive but not very [2] ________________ . They usually [3] ________________ black clothes and listen to Simple Plan, Fresno and Hateen.

There are also tribes of people [4] ________________ love hip hop. They love to listen to people like 50 cent and Eminem. They are really outgoing and love dancing, [5] ________________ is something they do really well.

All these differences make life much more interesting.

Adapted from: http://my3b.blogspot.com/

1 2 3 4 5 6

2 **Do YOU belong to a tribe? If so, describe it. If not, describe a tribe you admire.**

____

____

3 **Match the columns and find out who the mystery man is.**

1 What is his hair like?	[ ] He wears a suit and usually a bow tie.
2 What is he like?	[ ] It's short and white.
3 Where does he work?	[ ] He's overweight and wears glasses.
4 What does he wear?	[ ] He works on TV. He has a talk show.
5 What does he look like?	[ ] He's funny and very intelligent.

The mystery man is ________________________________ .

4 Rewrite the sentences using the words in parentheses.

1 I don't like the blue jeans. I like the black jeans.
(but / ones) I don't like the blue jeans but I like the black ones.

2 I got a new computer. It is much faster than my old computer.
(which / one) ______

3 I live in a nice area. There is no traffic there.
(where) ______

4 I lost my cell phone. Mom gave me a new cell phone.
(but / one) ______

5 We have a new teacher. He lived abroad for two years.
(who) ______

5 Think about **YOUR** routine. Use the prompts below and write sentences.

1 a place / you buy something — The Bakers is the place where I buy bread every day.
2 a person / you see every day ______
3 a place / you do something nice ______
4 a book / you sometimes read ______

6 Look at the pictures and give **YOUR** opinion.

1 Which tattoo do you prefer?
______

2 Which girl is more beautiful?
______

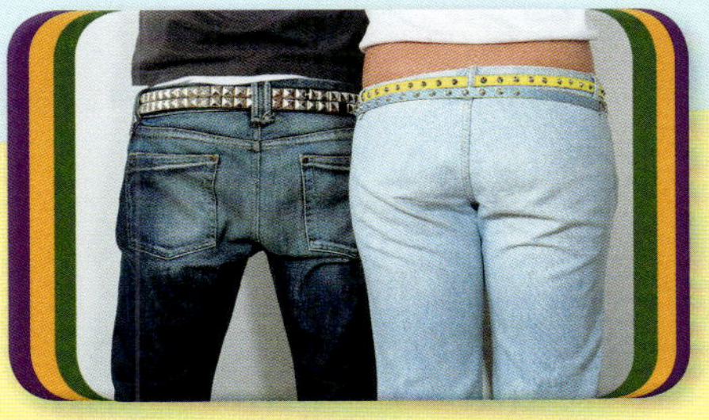

3 Which jeans would you buy?
______

4 Which clothes would you choose to wear?
______

Want more?
Go to Word Log U5 (p. 99)

Unit 6

It's all in your mind

Lesson 1

READING & COMPREHENSION

1 **Before answering the quiz below, learn the highlighted words and expressions with the help of your teacher or a dictionary. Take notes in your notebook.**

TEEN DREAM QUIZ

Hey Teens! Below you'll find SEVEN questions about dreams. Choose the best answer for each one, then take a look at the bottom of the page to view the answers.

1 **What is a dream? It's...**
1 an image of your future.
2 an image of something that you desire.
3 a little drama that our minds make up when we are asleep.

2 **How often do we dream per night?**
1 Once.
2 Four to six times.
3 Eight to ten times.

3 **Does everybody dream?**
1 No, only some people.
2 Yes, but some people don't remember their dreams.
3 Yes, but some people only have nightmares.

4 **Do dreams have any hidden meaning?**
1 No, they mean nothing.
2 Yes, they express our hidden desires.
3 Some are meaningful but others are only random images.

5 **If you dream about somebody, does it mean this person will dream about you too?**
1 Yes, because we are all psychically linked.
2 No, you were just thinking about the person.
3 Only if you just saw the person yesterday.

6 **If you dream about a person you have a crush on, it means you'll be together soon. Is it true?**
1 Yes, because why else would you dream about that person?
2 Yes, because by dreaming it, you are willing it to happen!
3 No, but dreaming it means you want it to happen.

7 **You keep having this one dream over and over: you are somewhere dark and spooky, but you know you have never been there. What does it mean?**
1 It doesn't mean anything really. Recurring dreams are very common.
2 It means that you will go there one day.
3 It means that you lived there in a past life.

Key: [1] 3; [2] 2; [3] 2; [4] 3; [5] 2; [6] 3; [7] 1.

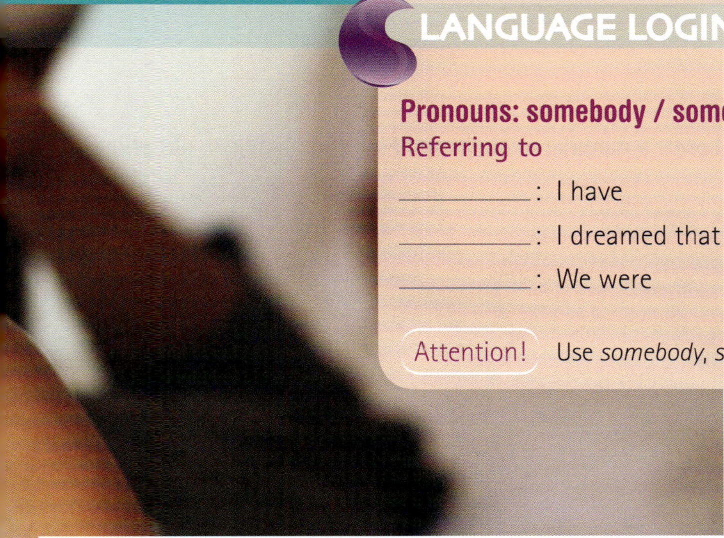

LANGUAGE LOGIN

Pronouns: somebody / someone, something & somewhere

Referring to

________:	I have	**something**	to tell you. It's about a dream I had.
________:	I dreamed that	**somebody / someone**	was following us.
________:	We were	**somewhere**	dark and spooky.

Attention! Use *somebody, someone, something* and *somewhere* in **positive** sentences.

2 **Do YOU usually remember your dreams? Do you have any recurring dreams?**

GO GET IT

somebody / someone, something & somewhere

3 **Look at the Language Login and complete the first column using the words below based on what the pronouns refer to.**

a place   a thing   a person

PRACTICE

4 **Learn more about dreams. Circle the correct option. Then listen and check your answers.**

26

Most Common Teen Dreams

Dream	Interpretation
Being chased	You might be trying to avoid **something / somewhere**: a fear or a relationship.
Being naked at school	You are not prepared for **someone / something**, like a test, and you feel exposed.
Failing a test	You are insecure about your abilities and worried that you may disappoint **somebody / somewhere** who is important to you.
Losing property	Losing **someone / something** means that you think a valuable aspect of your life is at risk.
Being lost	Being **somewhere / something** unknown or lost indicates that you feel vulnerable and inadequate.

5 **Complete the sentences with the pronouns from the Language Login.**

1 Children usually dream that there is ___something___ horrible under their beds.

2 A Where's Kay?
B She went ______________ to buy a present for her cousin.

3 Oh, no! ______________ has taken my bag! Let's call the police.

4 A corkscrew is ______________ that we use to open wine bottles.

5 I can't find my keys. They must be ______________ in my bedroom.

6 Did you hear the doorbell ring? I think there is ______________ at the door.

6 **Give your classmate THREE clues and three chances to guess what YOU are talking about. Use the pictures to help you or use your imagination.**

Example:
A It's somewhere where you can sleep.
B I know. A bedroom!
A No. It's somewhere where you can take a shower too.
B Hang on a minute. Somewhere where you can sleep and take a shower... Your home!
A No! Last chance. It's somewhere where you stay when you travel.
B I know now. A hotel.
A That's right!

Lesson 2

LISTENING & READING

1 **Read and listen to the dream narratives of three teenagers. There's a mistake in each one. Find the mistakes, underline and correct them.**

27

Ruth's dream

Last night I had that dream again. I dreamed that I was taking a geography test but I wasn't in my classroom. I was somewhere in a strange building and I didn't know anybody around me. When I looked at the test I realized I didn't know anything. I had a horrible feeling of panic and started to cry. The strange thing was that when I woke up I was actually crying.

1 Correction:

Keith's dream

For the past few months I've had a recurring dream. I'm always at the edge of a very high building and there is nobody there with me. I'm sitting there enjoying the view when suddenly someone comes from behind me and pushes me into the abyss. I fall through the air for a few minutes but I always wake up before I reach the ground.

2 Correction:

Heather's dream

Last night I had a very weird dream. I dreamed that I was at a dirty restaurant in Egypt, which is quite strange because I've never been there. I felt hungry so I ordered something to eat, but when I bit it I felt there was something hard inside it. I opened my mouth and my teeth started falling out in my hands. It was absolutely disgusting!

3 Correction:

COMPREHENSION

2 **Now match the texts with the pictures.**

3 **Read the dream narratives in #1 again and check (✓) the names of the teenagers who...**

	Ruth	Keith	Heather
1 had a nightmare last night.	✓		
2 have had recurring dreams.			
3 dreamed she lost her teeth.			
4 woke up crying last night.			
5 dreamed he was falling.			

4 **How often do YOU dream? Are they usually good dreams or nightmares?**

LANGUAGE LOGIN

Pronouns: some, any, no + body / thing / where / one

	Affirmate Sentences	Questions and Negative sentences	Affirmate Sentences (negative meaning)
People	There's **somebody** / **someone** at the door.	I didn't know **anyone** / ______ around me.	There is **no one** / ______ there with me.
Things	I ordered something to eat.	I realized I didn't know ______ .	There is **nothing** I can do.
Places	I was ______ in a strange building.	Did you go **anywhere** interesting?	There was **nowhere** for me to go.

Attention! Use *nobody, no one, nothing* and *nowhere* in **positive** sentences.
Use *anybody, anyone, anything* and *anywhere* in **questions** and **negative** sentences.

GO GET IT

some, any, no + body or one / thing / where

5 Look at the highlighted words in #1 and complete the sentences in the Language Login.

Tip
We do not usually use two negatives in a sentence.
We **don't say**: I did**n't** see ~~**nothing**~~.
We **say**: I did**n't** see **anything**.

PRACTICE

6 Last night Ruth woke up crying. Complete the conversation she had with her mother. Use the pronouns from the Language Login.

Debra Ruth, wake up, darling. Wake up.
Ruth Mom?
Debra Is there [1] anything happening, sweetie? I heard you crying.
Ruth [2] ______ serious, Mom. I just had a horrible nightmare.
Debra What about?
Ruth I was [3] ______ in an old building, I guess. There were lots of people there but I didn't know [4] ______ .
Debra What happened then?
Ruth [5] ______ gave me a piece of paper. It was a test and I didn't know [6] ______ .
Debra Oh, dear. You are just worried about school. I'll get you [7] ______ warm to drink.
Ruth Please, Mom, don't go [8] ______ .
Debra OK, sweetie. I'll stay here with you. Go back to sleep now.

LOG IN

7 Practice with a classmate.
Describe a strange, funny or frightening dream YOU've had. Use the questions below to help you.

1 Where were you?
2 Who were you with?
3 What happened?
4 How did you feel? Anxious? Scared? Sad? Happy?

Example:
A Where were you?
B Somewhere dark and crowded, maybe a theater or a movie theater.
A Who were you with?
B Nobody I know. They were strangers.

Want more?
Go to Grammar Log – G11 (p. 94)

READING & COMPREHENSION

1 Dr. Perry is a dream specialist. She has written many books about dreams. Read this extract from her latest book and answer the questions below.

28

Research has demonstrated that there are some dreams which are universal. This means that some dreams are common to different cultures and generations. The most common universal dream is the dream of being chased and attacked. Apparently, 80% of people have already had this sort of dream which is, in fact, a natural response to stress. Other very common dreams are dreams of falling, meeting a celebrity, being lost and being naked in public.

1 What are universal dreams?

____

2 What is the most common universal dream? What does it mean?

____

2 Have **YOU** ever had any of universal dreams listed in the article in #1? Which one(s)? How did you feel about it / them?

LISTENING

3 Listen to Dr. Perry being interviewed by a few students from an American university. Check (✓) the questions they ask her.

29

1 ◯ Universal dreams are common to different cultures and generations, aren't they?
◯ Are universal dreams common to different cultures and generations?

2 ◯ Is the most common universal dream the dream of being chased and attacked?
◯ The most common universal dream is the dream of being chased and attacked, isn't it?

3 ◯ Many people don't dream of being attacked, do they?
◯ Many people dream of being attacked, don't they?

4 ◯ You said last week that you often dream about meeting a celebrity, didn't you?
◯ You didn't say last week that you dreamed about meeting a celebrity, did you?

5 ◯ Have you ever dreamed about being naked in public too?
◯ You have never dreamed about being naked in public too, have you?

LANGUAGE LOGIN

Question tags

Affirmative Sentences

Your latest book **is** about dreams, **isn't it**?
You **dream** about being chased, **don't you**?
You **said** that last week, ______________________ ?
Dr. Perry **teaches** at a university, **doesn't she**?
You **have dreamed** about being naked, **haven't you**?
Dr. Perry **is going to be** at the conference, **isn't she**?
She **will give** a talk, **won't she**?

Negative Sentences

It **isn't** about traumas, **is it**?
You **don't have** nightmares, **do you**?
You **didn't say** that yesterday, **did you**?
She **doesn't teach** at high school, **does she**?
You **have never dreamed** about going to the moon, ____________ ?
But you **aren't going to be** there, **are you**?
The room **won't be** open before 9, **will it**?

Attention!

Question tags are formed with *auxiliary verbs*.
We use question tags to find out or confirm information.
The question tag for *I am* is *"aren't I?"*. Example: I'm the first person on the list, *aren't I?*

GO GET IT

question tags

4 **Look at the questions in #3. Find TWO question tags to complete the Language Login.**

5 **Study the Language Login. Complete the rules about question tags with *affirmative* and *negative*.**

If the first part of the sentence is *affirmative*, the question tag is [1] ______________________ .
If the first part of the sentence is *negative*, the question tag is [2] ______________________ .

PRACTICE

6 **Add question tags to these sentences. Pay attention to the auxiliaries and verb tenses.**

1 You are a psychologist, aren't you ?
2 Mark has never dreamed about marrying me, ______________ ?
3 Freud studied dreams, ______________ ?
4 Most people have dreams every night, ______________ ?
5 I'm in trouble, ______________ ?
6 You didn't have a nightmare last night, ______________ ?
7 You aren't worried about that dream, ______________ ?
8 Dr. Perry is a psychologist, ______________ ?
9 Dennis will contact Dr. Perry, ______________ ?
10 Peter isn't going to tell you about his dream, ______________ ?

LOG IN

7 **Practice with a classmate.**
Make THREE guesses about your partner. Check your guesses with question tags.

A You live in an apartment, don't you?
B Yes, I do. You have been to Argentina, haven't you?
A No, I haven't.

Want more?
Go to Grammar Log – G12 (p. 94)

Lesson 4

1 Read Martin Luther King's biography and answer the questions below.

30

Historic figures ›› Black history ›› Biography ›› Martin Luther King, Jr.

Martin Luther King, Jr.

A MAN WHO HAD A DREAM

January 15, 1929 – April 4, 1968
Nationality: American

'I have a dream that my four little children will one day live in a nation where they will not be judged by the color of their skin but by the content of their character.'
Martin Luther King

Martin Luther King Jr. was born on January 15, 1929 in Atlanta, Georgia. Martin was Reverend Martin Luther King and Alberta Williams King's second child, but their first son. The Kings' other children were Willie Christine and Alfred Daniel.

King attended segregated public schools in Georgia and graduated from Morehouse College with a degree in sociology in 1948. Then King moved to Boston and started his doctoral studies at Boston University. He received his Doctor of Philosophy (Ph.D.) in 1955. In Boston, King met Coretta Scott, a singer, and they got married. The couple had two sons and two daughters.

In the 1950's and 60's King worked as a pastor at a Baptist Church and became a social activist for civil rights. King followed a non-violent resistance method based on Gandhi's philosophy. In Washington D.C. in August 1963, Martin Luther King delivered his famous "*I Have a Dream*" speech. After the speech, King's ideal became a symbol of hope for African Americans who dreamed of equality in the USA. *Time* magazine named King "Man of the Year" and one year later, at the age of 35, he was awarded the Nobel Peace Prize.

Martin Luther King was assassinated on April 4, 1968 during a visit to Memphis, Tennessee.

Vocabulary Box

Segregated public schools = At that time in the USA the school system separated black and white people because of racial discrimination. A segregated school was the one that separated or isolated black people from others.

1 Where was Martin Luther King born? In Atlanta.
2 What did King's father do? ______
3 When did King graduate from college? ______
4 Who did King get married to? ______
5 How many chidren did Coretta and Martin Luther King have? ______
6 Which important prize was King awarded? ______

2 What do **YOU** think was Martin Luther King's dream? Read extracts from his speech and exchange ideas with your teacher and classmates. Do you share his dream?

"I have a dream that one day this nation will rise up and live out the true meaning of its creed: 'We hold these truths to be self-evident: that all men are created equal.'
I have a dream that one day on the red hills of Georgia the sons of former slaves and the sons of former slave owners will be able to sit down together at the table of brotherhood.
I have a dream that my four little children will one day live in a nation where they will not be judged by the color of their skin but by the content of their character."
Martin Luther King

(Extracts from "I Have a Dream" speech, available at www.usconstitution.net/dream.html)

Vocabulary Box

creed = a set of beliefs or principles
former = happening or existing before, but not now.

LANGUAGE LOGIN

Possessive 's – singular & plural

1 King had an ideal. → King**'s** ideal became a symbol of hope.
2 The Kings had three children. → The Kings**'** children were called Martin, Willie and Alfred.
3 Martin and Alberta had two sons. → Martin and Alberta**'s** sons were Martin Jr. and Alfred.
4 King and Kennedy were murdered. → King**'s** and Kennedy**'s** murders were a shock to America.

GO GET IT

possessive 's

3 Study the Language Login. Then read the sentences below and check (✓) the option which expresses the same idea.

1 Martin and Coretta had four cute kids together.
- ◯ *Martin's and Coretta's* four kids were cute.
- ◯ *Martin and Coretta's* four kids were cute.

2 Mandela and King received one Nobel Peace Prize each in different years.
- ◯ *Mandela's and King's* prizes were given in different years.
- ◯ *Mandela and King's* prizes were given in different years.

PRACTICE

4 Rewrite the sentences using the *possessive 's*.

1 King had a wife and she became an activist too.
King's ______________ wife became an activist too.

2 King and Gandhi taught us lessons that we will always remember.
______________________ lessons will always be remembered.

3 Kennedy had brothers and they were politicians too.
______________________ were politicians too.

4 Kennedy and Jacqueline had a son and he died in a plane crash.
______________________ son died in a plane crash.

5 *Doctors Without Borders* won the Nobel Peace Prize in 1999.
______________________ prize was given in 1999.

LOG IN

5 Writing.
Imagine YOU are a political leader and you are preparing a speech about your dreams for our society. In your notebook, write a short paragraph about your dreams. You can write about the topics below.

education health homeless people
jobs slums social rights prejudice

Example: *I have a dream. I have a dream that one day all children will have a comfortable home and will go to school every day because they won't have to work to help their parents. I have a dream that...*

Want more?
Go to Grammar Log – G13 (p. 95)

1 **What's going on in the situations below? Complete the sentences using *some*, *any*, *no* + *thing*, *where*, *body* / *one*.**

1

There's nothing to eat in the fridge.

2

He needs to go ______________ quiet.

3

He doesn't have ______________ to help him.

4

She can't find her MP3 player ______________ .

5

There's ______________ in the restaurant.

2 **Match each sentence with its corresponding *question tag*.**

1 You are from Belo Horizonte,
2 We can't eat or drink in the lab,
3 Grace has moved abroad,
4 The kids had their last class yesterday,
5 The bank doesn't open on Sundays,
6 You live near the river,

[ ] didn't they?
[ ] don't you?
[ ] aren't you?
[ ] does it?
[ ] can we?
[ ] hasn't she?

3 **Complete the sentences with the names of people YOU know. Then write a comment using the *possessive 's*.**

1 Gloria has an old car.
Gloria's car is really big and ugly.

2 ______________ has a son.
____

3 ______________ bought a new T-shirt.
____

4 ______________ have a dog.
____

5 ______________ has a child and ______________ has a child too.
____

4 Nate and Ruby are talking about their final tests. Complete their dialogue with *tag questions* and words from the box. TWO options will not be used.

somewhere anybody anywhere somebody

Nate Hey, Ruby. You know our finals start on Monday, [1] ______________ ?

Ruby Yeah, but I'm not really happy about it.

Nate Well, is [2] ______________ ever happy about exams? I don't think so. But you have started studying, [3] ______________ ?

Ruby Well, I've borrowed Lisa's notes and they really help. But I still feel I have so much to do!

Nate OK, I'll tell you what. Come and study with me this afternoon after school. We can cover at least one subject today, [4] ______________ ?

Ruby I guess. Do you want me to go [5] ______________ and buy some snacks?

Nate That sounds great. I'll meet you after school then.

5 How do YOU feel about tests? Answer the questions below.

1 Do you usually study alone for your tests? Why?

____

2 Do you eat anything while you study? What kind of thing do you eat?

____

3 Have you ever borrowed a friend's notes? Why?

____

6 Famous fairy tale characters also have people who worry about them! Complete the sentences below. Then decide who said those sentences.

1 I told you not to talk to ______________ on the way to your Grandma's house!
Little Red Riding Hood's mother.

2 How come you couldn't destroy that pig ____ house?
The wolf's ______________ .

3 You haven't lied again, ______________ ?
Pinocchio's ______________ .

4 Oh, no! You've eaten the witch ______ apple...
Snow White's ______________ .

Want more?
Go to Word Log U7 (p. 100)

Unit 7

Mind-boggling creations

Lesson 1

VOCABULARY WORK

computer technology

1 Match the words or expressions to their meanings.

1 online community	[ ]	to talk, to have a conversation.
2 3D	[1]	a group of people who have similar interests and meet in a virtual space.
3 avatar	[ ]	a place on the Internet where people can communicate by typing messages.
4 to chat	[ ]	a created virtual identity.
5 a chat room	[ ]	things that are produced to be sold and consumed, such as food or equipment.
6 tools	[ ]	having or seeming to have three dimensions: length, depth and height.
7 goods	[ ]	programs that you use to do things with a computer.

READING & COMPREHENSION

2 Read the webpage of *Teen Second Life* and check (✓) the correct alternatives. 31

1 *Teen Second Life* is...
- ◯ a video game.
- ◯ an online community for teenagers.
- ◯ a computer company.

2 *Teen Second Life* users...
- ◯ get things and land for free.
- ◯ compete against each other.
- ◯ choose a new identity.

3 *In Teen Second Life* teens...
- ◯ only interact with teens.
- ◯ can interact with teens and adults.
- ◯ never interact with adults.

3 Are YOU a member of *Teen Second Life*? What do you think about it?

TEEN SECOND LIFE

Teen Second Life: A Fantastic Virtual World

Teen Second Life is a 3D virtual online community where teens aged 13 to 17 make friends, play and learn. In *Teen Second Life* teenagers can create an "avatar", fly through a 3D landscape and chat with other teens from all over the world. *Teen Second Life* is much more than a video game or a chat program. *Teen Second Life* offers its users the tools and resources to build their own vision of a better world. The buildings are designed, vehicles are created and a virtual identity is chosen by the user. Then residents meet in different environments and social groups. But something is similar to real life: goods and land aren't given to you, you have to buy them.
Teen Second Life is developed by Linden Lab, a company based in San Francisco. This company provides the technology and guarantees online protection but it is the users who create the virtual world using their imagination.
Teen Second Life is a global community for teenagers so only teens will interact with other teens but occasionally teachers are brought in for special educational projects.
Join the community now and explore the *Teen Second Life* experience.

Adapted from http://teen.secondlife.com/ [Accessed August 2008]

LANGUAGE LOGIN

Present passive (aff. & neg.)

	Active voice	Passive voice
Affirmative	Linden Lab **develops** *Teen Second Life.* Users **create** vehicles.	Teen Second Life **is developed** by Linden Lab. Vehicles **are created**.
Negative	They **don't give** you land. They **don't give** you goods.	Land **isn't given** to you. Goods **aren't given** to you.

Attention! We use the **passive voice** when we don't know who does the action or it isn't important to mention it.

To form passive voice we use verb ______________ + the past participle.

GO GET IT

present passive (aff. & neg.)

4 **Look at the sentences in the Language Login and complete the rule.**

5 **Read the webpage in #2 again and underline the passive verbs.**

PRACTICE

6 **The sentences below are *passive*. Complete them using the *Past participle* of the verbs given.**

Communication and collaboration in the Information Age

create
make (2x)
send
upload
use
write (2x)

1 Millions of e-mails ___are written___ every day.
2 MSN Messenger ______________ worldwide by millions of people of all ages.
3 Text messages ______________ on cell phones and ______________ to relatives and friends.
4 Blogs ______________ to record personal activities and opinions.
5 Wikis ______________ collaboratively by many people.
6 About 50,000 video clips ______________ onto YouTube every day.
7 In the past, international phone calls were really expensive, but nowadays calls ______________ for practically nothing.

7 **Change the sentences below into the *Passive*. Find the *Past participle* forms in #2.**

In *Teen Second Life*...

1 people design buildings. ___buildings are designed.___
2 people create vehicles. ___vehicles___
3 people choose avatars. ______________
4 people buy land and goods. ______________
5 people bring in teachers for special projects.
____

8 **Write THREE sentences about YOU using the prompts below. Use the *Passive voice*. Follow the model.**

Example: I / wake up / by my parents
I am woken up by my parents. / I'm not woken up by my parents. I use an alarm clock.

1 I / take / school / by my parents
____

2 My pet / feed / by me
____

3 My bed / make / by my mom
____

Lesson 2

VOCABULARY WORK

video game production

1 **What do YOU know about video game production? Use words from the two boxes to write expressions related to the process of creating a video game. What are the possible combinations?**

animate create design draw scan sell test write

a story characters an environment sketches a product

____

____

____

LISTENING & COMPREHENSION

2 **Jason Parker is a video game designer. He is being interviewed on a TV show. Listen to the interview and number the stages of video game production in the order they happen.**

32

HOW A GAME IS MADE

1 The story is created.
2 The storyboard is organized.
3 The characters are drawn.
4 The sketch is animated.
5 The 3D environments are designed.
6 The code is written.
7 The game is tested.

3 **Would YOU like to be a game designer / tester? Why?**

LANGUAGE LOGIN

Present passive (int.)

Interrogative	Short answers
Is the story **created** by a designer?	**Yes**, it **is**. **No**, it **isn't**.
Are the games **tested**?	**Yes**, they **are**. **No**, they **aren't**.
How **is** a video game **made**?	

GO GET IT

present passive (int.)

4 **Study the Language Login to learn how to form questions in the *Passive voice*. Then complete the interview using the verbs in parentheses.**

1 *Pamela* How is a video game made, Jason? (make)

Jason First of all, the story is created.

2 *Pamela* ______ the story ______ by a writer? (create)

Jason No, it isn't. It is created by the game designer.

3 *Pamela* ______ the characters ______ by hand? (draw)

Jason Yes, they are.

PRACTICE

5 **Turn the affirmative sentences below into interrogative sentences.**

1 Video games are sold all over the world.

______

2 The sketches are animated.

______

3 The code is written last.

______

6 **Did YOU play with LEGOs® when you were a kid? Read the text below and make up the questions for an interview with one of the project managers of the LEGO® group.**

Approximately 19 billion LEGO® elements are produced every year and are bought by 400 million children and adults. LEGO® bricks are made in a simple way. The plastic is heated to 232ºC and then it is injected into molds at a very high pressure. It takes seven seconds to cool and eject the new elements. The molds used are so accurate that only 18 elements in every million produced are rejected for bad quality. All LEGO® elements are analized to see if they are fully functional.

Interviewer How long have you worked with LEGO®?

Manager For five years. It's a great place to work.

Interviewer Tell us, [1] are many LEGO® elements produced every year?

Manager Yes, more than 19 billion.

Interviewer [2] ______

Manager Yes, they are. 400 million people of all ages buy LEGO®.

Interviewer Tell us about the process of producing LEGO®.

[3] ______

Manager The plastic is heated and then it is injected into molds.

Interviewer [4] ______

Manager No, only 18 elements in a million. Isn't that amazing?

Interviewer It sure is! Thanks a lot.

Based on "The Making of... a LEGO®" by Joseph Pisani. Available online at www.businessweek.com (August 2008) and www.popandco.com/archive/moab/ (August 2008)

LOG IN

7 **Practice with a classmate.**
Interview your classmate. Use the prompts below.

be influenced by your friends / parents / teachers
be pressured by your parents / teachers
be bullied by your classmates / older brother / sister
be embarrassed by your grandparents / parents / friends

Example:
A Are you influenced by your friends?
B Yes, I think I am. Are you?
A No, I'm not. I think I'm influenced by my parents.

Lesson 3

READING & COMPREHENSION

1 **Read the magazine article about the invention of three popular products. Find out which products they are and complete the descriptions.**

33

Three accidental inventions that changed the world

[1] ______________________® notes were invented around 1970 when Spencer Silver was working in the 3M research laboratories trying to find a strong adhesive. Instead of a strong adhesive the new formula was too weak – it stuck to objects but could be easily lifted off. One day Arthur Fry, a 3M workmate and member of a church choir, needed bookmarks for his church hymnal and remembered Silver's adhesive.

[2] ______________________® was invented in 1886 in Atlanta, Georgia, when pharmacist John Pemberton decided to change the formula for a headache medicine, using sugar instead of wine. By mistake John's assistant added carbonated water to the syrup and this produced a fizzy drink. John thought it was 'delicious and refreshing'.

[3] ______________________ were invented in 1853 by George Crum, an American chef at an elegant resort in Saratoga Springs, New York. One day a dinner guest found Crum's French fries too thick and rejected the order. Angry Crum then decided to make fries that were too thin to eat with a fork but, to his surprise, the customer was very happy. Soon other guests started requesting Crum's fries too.

2 **Read the article in #1 again and check (✓) the correct answers.**

Which product was invented...

	Post-it	Coca-Cola	Potato chips
by mistake?	✓		
in the 19th century?			
in the 20th century?			
by one person only?			
by two people?			

3 **What do YOU think are the most important inventions ever made? Why?**

LANGUAGE LOGIN

Past passive (aff., neg. & int.)

Affirmative
Coca-Cola® **was invented** by accident.
Potato chips **were made** by accident.

Negative
Coca-Cola® **wasn't produced** with alcohol.
Post-it® notes **weren't invented** on purpose.

Interrogative
Were Post-it® notes **created** in 1980?
Were they **created** in 1970?

Short answers
No, they **weren't**.
Yes, they **were**.

GO GET IT

past passive

4 Look at the sentences in the Language Login and complete the sentences below with the *Passive* form of the verbs in parentheses.

1 The first LEGO® bricks were made (make) of wood.
2 The first video game ______ (call) *Tennis for Two* and it ______ (create) in 1958.
3 A When ______ the Barbie doll ______ (create)?
B In 1959. It ______ (create) by a woman whose daughter was called Barbara.
4 Nuclear energy ______ (not invent) to produce domestic electricity. It ______ (invent) to produce a bomb.

PRACTICE

5 Change the sentences below from the *Active voice* to the *Passive voice*.

Coca-Cola®

1 John Pemberton invented a new formula.
A new formula was invented by John Pemberton.
2 Pemberton added sugar to the formula.
______ to the formula.
3 He produced a new and refreshing drink in 1886.
______ in 1886.

Post-it®

4 Arthur Fry used the adhesive as a bookmark.
______ as a bookmark.

Potato chips

5 The dinner guest rejected Crum's fries in New York.
______ in New York.
6 Crum sliced the potatoes thin.
______ thin.

6 Use the prompts below to write questions and answers about the inventions in #1.

1 Coca-Cola® / invent / the USA?
Was Coca-Cola® invented in the USA? Yes, it was.
2 Coca-Cola® / invent / 20th century?
______ ______
3 Post-it® notes / invent / by 3M?
______ ______
4 Potato chips / invent / the French?
______ ______

LOG IN

7 Practice with a classmate.
Ask and answer about when YOU think the inventions below were created. Use question tags. Then check your answers with your teacher.

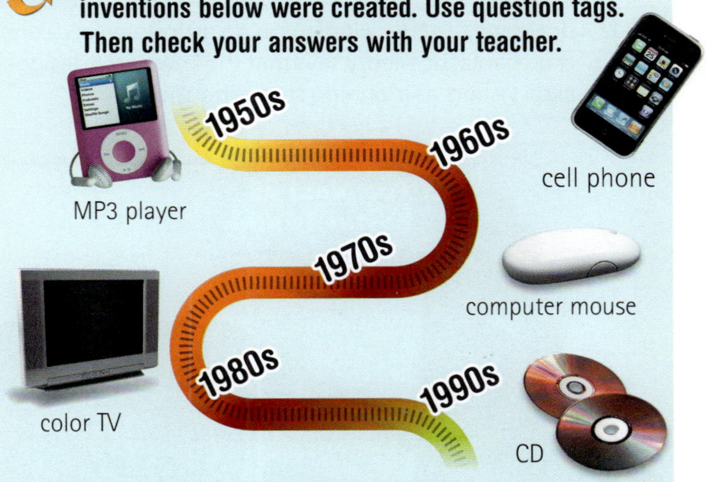

A The color TV was invented in the 1960s, wasn't it?
B I think so. / I don't think so. I think it was invented in the 1950s.

Tip
In the 1980s.
We can say: *In the nineteen eighties* or *In the eighties.*

READING & COMPREHENSION

1 **Read the webpage and answer the questions.**

34

GET YOUR ANSWER

ASK

ANSWER

Enter your question here

GO

Q: How were the moai carved and transported?

Moai are huge statues of human heads on Easter Island. The moai have puzzled archeologists and visitors since the first European explorers arrived on the island in 1722. How were these gigantic statues carved and transported? Some say they were built by Peruvian people because of their similarity to Incan stonework. Others say they were built by Polynesian groups who lived on the island and were extraordinarily good at making sailing canoes and massive stone structures. There is even a theory that suggests that a small group of "intelligent beings" from outer space taught the natives to make "robot-like" statues. Who has the answer?

Q: How were the Nazca lines drawn?

The famous Nazca lines of Peru, which lie across the Nazca desert, are an enigma. The drawings of animals, plants, objects and geometrical figures can only be fully seen from the air and how they were made remains a mystery. Since their discovery in the 1920's, they have inspired fantastic explanations. One of the theories says that the lines were drawn by the Nazca Indians as an astronomical calendar. A more fantastic theory says that the lines were designed by alien visitors as a landing strip. Who knows?

1. What are moai?
   ____
2. Where are they found?
   ____
3. When were the moai discovered?
   ____
4. What do the Nazca lines look like?
   ____
5. When were the Nazca lines discovered?
   ____

The Moai of Easter Island

Humming bird Nazca line

2 **What is YOUR explanation for the moai and the Nazca lines?**

VOCABULARY WORK

categories

3 **Cross out the words that do not belong to the group.**

1 mystery – enigma – puzzle – explorer
2 huge – massive – carved – gigantic
3 Inca – alien – outer space – UFO

4 **Look at the groups of words in #3 and say which group refers to...**

[ ] size
[ ] things you don't know how to explain
[ ] extraterrestial life

Lesson 4

LANGUAGE LOGIN

Passive with & without *by*

Active	Passive
The Peruvian people built the statues.	The statues were built **by** the Peruvian people.
The Nazca Indians drew the lines.	The lines were drawn **by** the Nazca Indians.

Attention! The *by- phrases* are used in the passive when it's more important to show *who* did the action than *what* the action was.
The highway was completed in 1980. ➜ probably by the engineers, but this is not relevant.
The table was made of wood. ➜ probably by the carpenter, but the material is more relevant.

GO GET IT

passive with & without by

5 **Read the Language Login carefully. Then cross out the by- phrases that are not necessary in the sentences below.**

1 The Nazca lines were seen from the plane by the passengers.
2 The lines were built by aliens as a landing place.
3 The tourists were taken by the driver to the Nazca lines site.
4 The idea that the Nazca lines formed an airfield for alien aircrafts was proposed by James W. Moseley in 1955.

PRACTICE

6 **Make sentences in the *Passive voice* using the prompts below. Decide if you need to include *by*... or not.**

1 Stonehenge / build (Neolithic people)
Stonehenge was built by the Neolithic people.

2 Tourists / take / to Stonehenge (the tourist guide)
____

3 *Mona Lisa* / paint (Leonardo da Vinci)
____

4 Some paintings / steal / from The Louvre (thieves)
____

5 airplane / invent / Santos Dumont
____

LOG IN

7 **Writing.**
Imagine YOU want to answer the following question on the GET YOUR ANSWER website: *What do you know about Machu Picchu?*
Use the information below and write a paragraph about it in your notebook. First read the example about the Palace of Versailles carefully.

The Palace of Versailles:

- built / Louis XIII
- expand / Louis XIV
- declare / the official residence of the Court of France / May 6, 1682
- the terrace / transform into / the Hall of Mirrors / from 1678 to 1684
- the Hall of Mirrors / build / to the glory of Louis XIV
- Le Brun / ordered / to design 30 compositions showing the king in different costumes

The Palace of Versailles **was built** by Louis XIII and **was expanded** by Louis XIV. The Palace **was declared** the official residence of the Court of France in May 6, 1682. The terrace **was transformed** into the Hall of Mirrors from 1678 to 1684. The Hall of Mirrors **was built** to the glory of Louis XIV. Le Brun **was ordered** to design 30 compositions showing the king in different costumes.

Based on www.chateauversailles.fr

Historic Santuary of Machu Picchu:

- Pre-Columbian Inca site
- located 2,400 meters above sea level
- 1400s – built by the Incas
- abandoned when Spanish invaders conquered the Inca Empire
- 1911 – rediscovered by explorer Hiram Bingham
- 1981 – declared a Historical Sanctuary
- one of the New Seven Wonders of the World

Machu Picchu is a pre-Columbian Inca site. It...

Want more?
Go to Grammar Log – G14 (p. 95)

1 **Do YOU know how a comic strip is produced? Complete the text below with the verbs in parentheses, using both the *Active* and the *Passive voices.***

Producing a cartoon strip may be easier than you think. First you [1] ______________ (create) the characters, which may be based on real people or not. When the characters are ready, the story [2] ______________ (write) and the whole environment [3] ______________ (design). Then you [4] ______________ (draw) some sketches and [5] ______________ (test) your product with a small group of consumers before you finally start selling it! And be ready for success!

2 **Read the online article about Mauricio de Souza, the creator of *Turma da Mônica*. Then answer the questions.**

Brazilian Celebrities

Mauricio de Souza was born in São Paulo, Brazil, in 1935. He created his first comic strip in 1959. Franjinha and his dog Bidu were the first characters. In the following 10 years, Cebolinha and Chico Bento joined them and were published in more than 200 different newspapers. Mônica, his most famous character, was created in 1970, when comics became popular all over the country. In the 70's, Mauricio developed a team of people who have been working with him ever since. Dolls, books, DVDs and all sorts of other products were designed by them and sold in Brazil and his comics were published in various countries. In the 80's, Mauricio opened *Black and White*, a studio with over seventy designers, where eight animation movies were produced. After some years, the studio closed because of economic difficulties. Mauricio decided to concentrate on merchandising and on the most important thing: comics. After all, Mônica and Cebolinha need lots of attention and care.

Adapted from www.monica.com.br

1 Were Mônica and Cebolinha created at the same time?

____

2 Was *Black and White* opened because of economic difficulties?

____

3 Were his animation movies produced only by him?

____

3 **Now answer about YOU.**

1 Are you a *Turma da Mônica* fan? ______________________________

2 Who was your favorite cartoon character when you were a kid? ______________________________

3 Do you read comics nowadays? Which ones? ______________________________

4 Who is your favorite cartoon character now? Why? ______________________________

4 **Japanese animation and comic books are extremely popular among teens. Match the columns to make complete sentences and find out more about an Anime convention in the USA.**

1 Dedicated fans of "anime" and "manga"...
2 They are known as "otaku" and go to these conventions...
3 At the convention, monologues and sketches...
4 *Shonen Jump* was designed to be the magazine...
5 The American version of the magazine...
6 The original Japanese version...

[ ] read by teens who adopt an anime lifestyle.
[ ] sells three million copies every week in Japan.
[ ] based on themes from manga and anime are performed by cosplays.
[1] got together at an Anime USA convention in northern Virginia.
[ ] was promoted and sold during the convention.
[ ] dressed in costumes based on their favorite characters and stories.

Adapted from: www.npr.org

5 **Copy the words next to their definitions.**

manga
anime
otaku
cosplays

1 Japanese animation, both on TV and in movies: ______
2 Serious fans of Japanese comics and animation: ______
3 Japanese comic books: ______
4 Fans who dress like their favorite characters: ______

6 **Rewrite the following sentences in the *Passive voice*.**

1 A few years ago, TV channels brought Pokémon cartoons to the USA.

______

2 The American version of *Shonen Jump* reflects the lifestyle of anime fans.

______

7 **Do YOU read manga? Why? Which one is your favorite?**

______

Want more?
Go to Word Log U7 (p. 100)

Unit 8

From mind to matter

Lesson 1

READING & COMPREHENSION

1 **Read and answer: what is the poster about?**

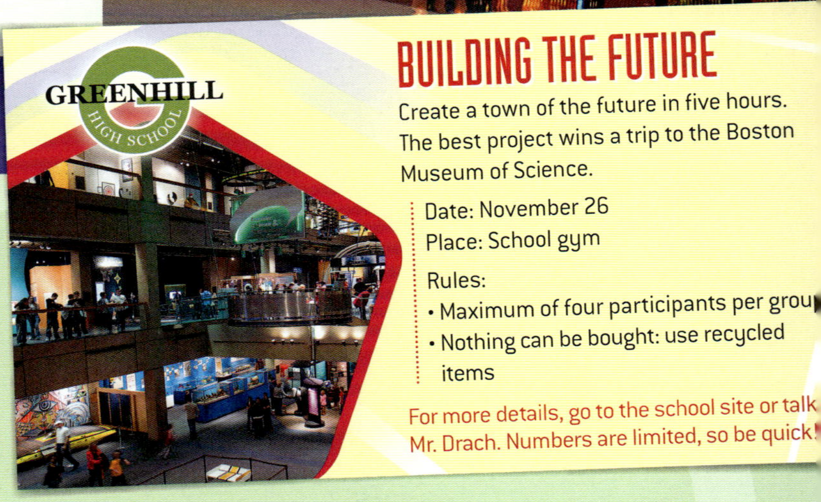

2 **Maya and Ethan, students at Greenhill High, are talking about the competition. Read their conversation and complete the sentences using the correct names: Maya, Ethan, Megan and Jasmine.**

35

Maya Are you going to take part in the competition?

Ethan What competition?

Maya Haven't you seen the poster? It's all over the school. I have one here. Look. Megan and I have already signed up for it. We're going to meet this weekend to plan our project. Do you want to join our group?

Ethan All right then.

Maya Great. I'll call Megan right away and tell her. We've planned to meet at my place on Saturday afternoon. Can you come too?

Ethan Sure. I'll think of lots of ideas before then. Hey, why don't we ask Jasmine to join us too? She's really creative, you know...

Maya Good idea, Ethan. I'm going to see her in a few minutes and then I'll ask her. I bet Jasmine will join us, you know, because of you.

Ethan Really? Do you think so?

Maya I'm positive. I've got to go. I'll tell Mr. Drach we have a group.

Ethan Sure! Right. OK.

1 ____________ didn't know about the competition.
2 ____________ hasn't signed up for the competition yet.
3 ____________ and ____________ have already started a group.
4 Ethan wants ____________ to be part of the group too.
5 Jasmine is interested in ____________ .

Tip

We write:	We can say:
Do you want to...?	Do you wanna...?
I've got to go.	Gotta go.

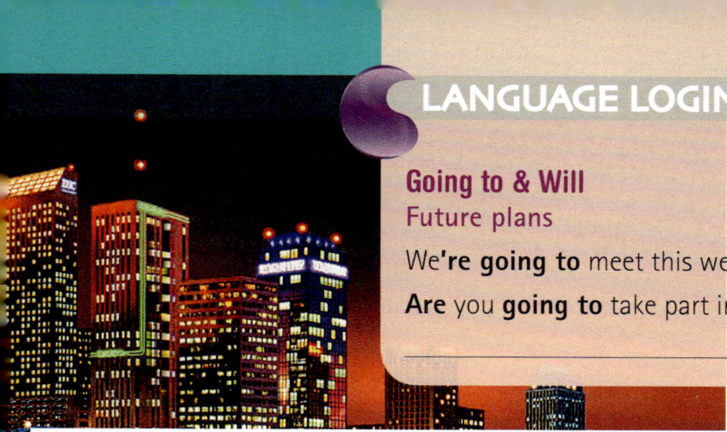

LANGUAGE LOGIN

Going to & Will

Future plans

We**'re going to** meet this weekend.

Are you **going to** take part in the competition?

____

Spontaneous decisions

I**'ll** call Megan right away.

____

I**'ll** tell Mr. Drach we have a group.

GO GET IT

going to & will

3 **Check (✓) the correct option.**

1 Maya says, *"I'll call Megan right away".*
- ◯ Maya has already planned to call Megan.
- ◯ Maya decided at that moment to call Megan.

2 Maya says, *"We're going to meet this weekend".*
- ◯ Maya has already planned the meeting.
- ◯ Maya decided at that moment to have a meeting.

Now complete the Language Login with the highlighted sentences from the dialogue in #2. Do they refer to future plans or to spontaneous decisions?

PRACTICE

4 **Complete the speech bubbles with *will* or *going to*.**

1 Don't cry. Give it to me and I ____________ mend it for you.

2 We ____________ get married next month.

3 That bag must be heavy. I ____________ help you carry it.

4 Sorry, I can't go out this afternoon. I ____________ study for my math test.

5 **Complete the dialogues using the verbs given and *will* or *going to*.**

1 A Oh... I forgot to give Ella her invitation.
  B Don't worry. I ____________ (see) her tomorrow. I ____________ (give) it to her.

2 A We ____________ (get) the train at 9 a.m. tomorrow morning.
  B I ____________ (give) you a ride to the station if you want.

3 A Chris ____________ (have) a birthday party tomorrow.
  B I know. Trish and I ____________ (buy) her present this afternoon. Do you want to come with us?

Want more?
Go to Grammar Log – G15 (p. 96)

Lesson 2

VOCABULARY WORK

do or make

1 ***Do* or *make*? With the help of your teacher or a dictionary, write the words in the correct column.**

a decision	a favor
a mistake	a phone call
arrangements	business
plans	the housework
your best	your homework

DO	MAKE
a favor	a decision

2 **Read these tips for teens and check (✓) the correct options.**

1 After ◯ **doing** ◯ **making** your homework, always check that you haven't ◯ **done** ◯ **made** silly mistakes.
2 Occasionally offer to ◯ **do** ◯ **make** the housework. This always keeps you in favor with Mom and Dad.
3 When you ◯ **do** ◯ **make** a call to a friend, try not to spend hours on the phone.
4 If you are ◯ **doing** ◯ **making** arrangements to go out with friends, let your parents know.
5 You can't always be perfect, but always try to ◯ **do** ◯ **make** your best.

READING & COMPREHENSION

3 **Ethan and Maya are chatting online and making arrangements. Read their conversation and complete the list to show what the abbreviations / slangs they use stand for.**

Chat

Ethan says: Hi. What's up?
Maya says: Doing my homework! ☹
Ethan says: R u going out l8er?
Maya says: No. Jasmine is coming here
Ethan says: Jas! ☺
Maya says: Yeah. We've made plans. We're having a girls' night in
Ethan says: So I can't go ☹
Maya says: No, Ethan. Not 2nite. But I'm seeing her again 2moro. We're going ice sk8ing. Wanna come?
Ethan says: Sure! Tom and I are playing soccer in the morning, but I'm not doing anything after lunch. What time?
Maya says: Let me text her to confirm
Ethan says: OK. I'll w8.
Maya says: We're meeting at 3 in front of the ice rink
Ethan says: OK. I'll be there. I just texted Tom. He's coming too
Maya says: Cool! I have to get back to my homework now
Ethan says: BFN ☺

1 R u Are you
2 l8er later
3 2nite ______
4 2moro ______
5 sk8ting ______
6 w8 ______
7 BFN ______
8 Wanna come? ______

4 **Read their conversation again and write T for *true* and F for *false*. Then correct the false sentences.**

1 [F] Ethan and Maya are texting each other.
No, they aren't. They are chatting online.
2 [ ] Maya is going out tonight.
3 [ ] Tom and Ethan are playing soccer tomorrow morning.
4 [ ] Jasmine is going ice skating tomorrow morning.
5 [ ] Maya is meeting Ethan at 3 p.m. tomorrow.
6 [ ] Maya is doing her homework.

GO GET IT

present continuous for future arrangements

5 Which of the sentences in #4 refer to:

1 actions that are in progress? 1 and ______

2 future arrangements 2, ______ and ______

6 Look at the Language Login and check (✓) the correct option.

The sentences in the Language Login refer to:

◯ actions that are in progress

◯ future arrangements

LANGUAGE LOGIN

Present continuous for future arrangements

Affirmative

We**'re having** a girls' night in.
I**'m seeing** her again tomorrow.
Tom and I **are playing** soccer in the morning.

Negative

I**'m not doing** anything after lunch.
Ethan **isn't meeting** Maya tonight.

Interrogative

Are you **going out** tonight?
Is he **doing** anything tomorrow?

PRACTICE

7 Look at Maya's diary for next week. Then complete the sentences to talk about her future arrangements. Use the *Present continuous* with future meaning in the correct form: affirmative or negative. Use the verbs in parentheses.

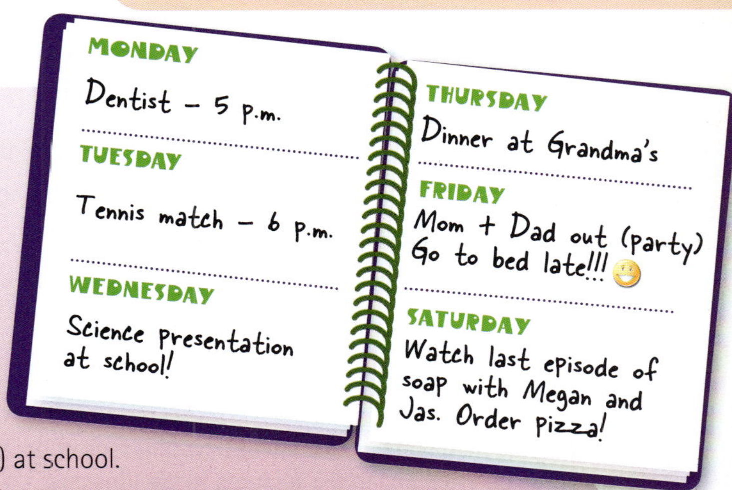

1 On Monday at 5 p.m. she is going (go) to the dentist.

2 On Tuesday evening she isn't playing (play) soccer.

3 On Wednesday she ______ (give) at school.

4 On Thursday ______ (have) at her Grandma's house.

5 On Friday her mom and dad ______ (stay) at home and she ______ (go) to bed early.

6 On Saturday night she and her friends ______ (watch) the last episode of the soap opera. They ______ (order) Chinese food. They ______ (order) pizza.

8 Use the actions below to help you complete the diary with YOUR future plans. Write FIVE sentences.

- play (something: tennis, soccer etc.)
- go (somewhere: to the beach, to a party, to the mall, to the movies etc.)
- watch TV
- visit (somebody, a museum)
- stay (at home, in bed)
- go out (with somebody)
- meet (somebody)

Want more?

Go to Grammar Log – G16 (p. 96)

	Saturday	Sunday
Morning	______	______
Afternoon	______	______
Evening	______	______

1 ______

2 ______

3 ______

4 ______

5 ______

VOCABULARY WORK

multi-word verbs

1 **Read these questions and then match the multi-word verbs to their definitions.**

◯ Is it difficult for you to *switch off* your cell phone and forget about it?
◯ Are you often worried that you cell phone battery might *run out*? And if it happens, do you get really angry?
◯ Do you *work out* at the gym or at home almost every day?

1 switch off [ ] be used completely
2 run out [ ] exercise to improve your strength
3 work out [ ] disconnect, make something stop working

Lesson 3

2 **Now read these other questions and try to remember the meaning of the highlighted multi-word verbs. Check (✓) the questions in #1 and #2 to which YOU would answer *yes*.**

◯ Would you find it practically impossible to give up the Internet for a week?
◯ When you get a computer, do you go on and find it difficult to stop using it?
◯ When you get up in the morning, do you go straight to the computer?
◯ When you travel, do you miss your gym and want to get back to it ASAP?

Vocabulary Box
ASAP = As soon as possible

READING & COMPREHENSION

3 **Read this magazine article about new illnesses of the modern non-stop culture we live in. Then match the pictures to the illnesses.**

36

24/7 Culture And Your Health

Younger generations seem to be living life faster than any previous generations and this is not good news! The 24/7 culture (24 hours per day, 7 days per week) can cause health problems. This culture might bring with it some bizarre new problems and symptoms as shown below.

1 Nomophobia

This is the fear of being out of cell phone contact. Research shows that approximately one in ten people feel anxious when their phone is switched off. They feel they need to be contactable at all times. In fact, research shows that running out of battery or accidentally leaving their cell phones at home can cause people more stress than traditionally stressful situations such as taking final exams.

2 Athletica Nervosa

People can become addicted to exercising and the natural chemical endorphin high they get after working out. This is most common in men and particularly those who read sports magazines. Often they are hit by the desire to look as good as the incredibly good-looking models they see and so become anxious about their own bodies.

3 Technoholic

Research shows that a worrying 33 per cent of us are becoming addicted to the Internet. Too much exposure to the Net can cause a break down in relationships. Often people spend more time using their technology than really socializing and this is not good. You may have dozens of cyber friends, but how many real ones can you count?

Based on www.timesonline.co.uk; http://en.wikipedia.org/wiki/Nomophobia [Accessed 8/08/08]

Now go back to #1 and #2. If you have checked three or more questions, YOU could be a victim of the so called 24/7 culture. Watch out!!

LANGUAGE LOGIN

Giving advice

If I were you, I'd buy a Smartphone.

If ________________, **I wouldn't** worry so much.

You ________________ stop checking your e-mail every five minutes.

You ________________ work less and relax more.

You **shouldn't** take a steroid supplement: they are really dangerous!

4 **For each picture in #3, check (✓) the advice that best helps people slow down.**

PICTURE 1

1 ◯ You should always take two cell phones with you wherever you go.

2 ◯ If I were you, I wouldn't worry so much about people and things at the other end of the phone.

PICTURE 2

1 ◯ You shouldn't be so worried about your physical appearance!

2 ◯ You ought to take a steroid supplement. Soon you will look like Mr. Universe!

PICTURE 3

1 ◯ If I were you, I'd buy a Smartphone. Then you can access Internet whenever you like.

2 ◯ You ought to find something else that interests you. For example, join a gym or take a painting course.

GO GET IT

giving advice

5 **Look at sentences in #4 and underline the different expressions used for giving advice. Then complete the Language Login.**

6 **Give some advice to Mitch, a 16-year-old who is suffering from stress. Read what he says and respond using the prompts given.**

1 *Mitch* I'm really upset. I got a 95% on my math test! I wanted 100%!

You (be happy / celebrate) Come on, Mitch. If I were you, I'd be really happy! Ninety-five percent is a great grade. You should celebrate!

2 *Mitch* I can't sleep. I keep thinking of the things I have to do the next day.

You (worry / relax) ________________

3 *Mitch* I'll never stop working out! I want a strong body.

You (become addicted to / take a break) ________________

4 *Mitch* I'm in love with a girl I met in a virtual chatroom but I'm afraid to meet her in person.

You (be afraid / live life for real) ________________

LOG IN

7 **Practice with a classmate.**
Talk about situations that make YOU stressed. Listen to your classmate and give advice on how to keep cool. Check the suggested topics for you to talk about.

bad weather | bullies | tests
rules from your parents
too many activities in a single day

Example:
A I hate tests. They make me feel nervous.
B You ought to think of tests as an exercise. You should get prepared but you shouldn't worry so much.
A True. But it is difficult.

Want more?
Go to Grammar Log – G17 (p. 97)

1 Are YOU optimistic or pessimistic about the future in ten years? Circle the appropriate words to give your opinion.

1 There will be **more / fewer** jobs available.
2 Our lives will be **more / less** stressful.
3 There will be **more / less** crime.
4 There will be **more / fewer** illnesses.
5 People will have **more / less** leisure time.

READING & COMPREHENSION

2 Read the introduction to the forum discussion about future gadgets and underline SEVEN objects that can be found in our homes.

37

Vocabulary Box

faucet = 

gadget = a small, cleverly designed machine or tool

Lesson 4

An amazing futuristic house is now on show in New York. The house is packed with lots of cool gadgets to help make our lives easier and reduce stress. For example, there are faucets which pour out smells instead of water. There is a mirror which, as well as showing your reflection, gives you the weather forecast, and there is a computer inside the fridge which gives information on the quality of the food being stored there. But this house is not just for gadget fans, the house is environmentally friendly too. It can tell how much energy you're using and warn you if a faucet has been left running or if you've left the air conditioner on too long. And it even has a water-powered alarm clock by the bed to wake you up in the morning!

Use your imagination and think about gadgets that you would like to have in the future. If you could have a cool gadget in your home, what would it be? Maybe a robot that makes your bed for you? What about an ice cream maker that knows what flavor you're thinking of?

YOUR COMMENTS

Carol, 15, Boston
I would like a special bed that lets me get eight hours sleep in ten minutes. If I had more time, I would be able to play on the computer more! At the moment I only seem to have time to study and go to school!

Gabriel, 15, Florida
If I could have a cool gadget in my home, I would have a special chair which takes me anywhere in the house automatically. On the right arm there would be a panel with lots of buttons for all the rooms in the house. You press the button and... whoosh... you are taken to that room.

Lauren, 13, Milford
I would like a pencil with e-mail, MSN and an MP4 player in it that would let me talk to my friends in secret. It would be so cool. If Mom or Dad came into my room, I would simply pretend that I was studying.

Joshua, 14, New York
I'd like a special robot that would clean my room for me. Mom and I always argue because of the mess in my room. Just imagine if a robot cleaned my room every day, Mom wouldn't shout at me all the time!

3 Now read "Your Comments" in #2. Give YOUR opinion about all the different gadgets mentioned.

1 Which gadgets mentioned do you think are:
good ideas? ______________________________
silly ideas? ______________________________

2 Which of the gadgets do you think:
might actually exist in the future? ______________________________
will never exist? ______________________________

GO GET IT

second conditional

4 **Look at the Language Login and complete the sentences using the words below.**

could would cleaned wouldn't

PRACTICE

5 **Match the columns to make full sentences.**

1 If I could have a robot,
2 If people could read thoughts,
3 I would be really tired after a couple of days,
4 If you could change one part of your body,
5 We would travel together,

[ ] they would be surprised.
[ ] if our parents allowed us.
[ ] it would clean my bedroom for me.
[ ] if I could do everything I wanted.
[ ] what would it be?

6 **Use the prompts to complete the questions.**

1 If _you could live_ (you / can live) anywhere in the world, which country _would you choose_ (you / choose)?
2 What ______ (you / do) if ______ (you / have) more free time?
3 If ______ (you / win) $10,000, what ______ (you / buy)?
4 If ______ (you / design) the love of your life, what ______ (he / she / look like)?

Now create YOUR own question.

If... ______

LANGUAGE LOGIN

Second conditional: *If I* + past tense + *I would...*

An imaginary situation

If + past tense

If I **had** more time,...
If a robot ______ my room every day, ...
If Mom or Dad **came** into my room, ...
If you ______ **have** a cool gadget, ...

The result

would(n't)...

... I **would be** able to play more on the computer.
... Mom ______ **shout** at me all the time.
... I ______ **pretend** that I was studying.
... what **would** it **be**?

Attention! The sentences describe *an imaginary situation.*

7 **Now give YOUR answers to the questions in #6.**

1 ______
2 ______
3 ______
4 ______

LOG IN

8 **Writing.**
If YOU could have a cool gadget, what would it be? In your notebook, write your description to send to the forum discussion on page 84. Check the Language Login again and include at least one sentence in the *second conditional*.

Want more?
Go to Grammar Log – G18 (p. 97)

Review

1 **Megan and her mother are talking about their vacation. Complete their dialogue with the verbs in parentheses in the correct future form – *Going to*, *Will* or *Present continuous*.**

Megan Mom, I was thinking... You [1] ______ (spend) summer vacations with Aunt Sylvia, right?

Ms. Moore In fact, WE are, darling. Why?

Megan Well, I thought you could let me do something else. Kate and Ray [2] ______ (hike) together this summer and...

Ms. Moore Ray? He's not even a close friend. I don't know, Megan. I [3] ______ (think) about it, OK?

Megan But Mom, Kate is my best friend. You know her parents and I would stay at her place for the summer. Come on, Mom.

Ms. Moore Listen, Megan, we haven't seen your Aunt Sylvia since she moved to Canada. She [4] ______ (arrive) after lunch and we [5] ______ (meet) her at the airport. Sylvia and I have been planning this trip together for a long time – for the three of us. The reason why my sister is coming over is YOU, darling. She misses you and she is dying to be with you. She has made all the arrangements. She told me we [6] ______ (stay) at a great hotel and that she [7] ______ (do) anything you want.

Megan Great! So maybe she [8] ______ (let) me go hiking with my friends.

Ms. Moore That's not fair, Megan. We [9] ______ (discuss) this later and I'm sure we [10] ______ (find) a way to please everybody. The secret word Megan is "compromise".

Megan All right!

2 **Ms. Moore doesn't know what to do. She loves Megan, but she knows Aunt Sylvia will be very disappointed if Megan doesn't stay with them. Complete the sentences below giving Ms. Moore some advice.**

1 Ms. Moore, if I ______

2 You should ______

3 You ought to ______

4 ______

3 **How do YOU think the situation was solved?**

______

4 Megan doesn't know what is going to happen next summer, but she has lots of ideas about the future. Read her blog entry. Use the words in the box to complete the text.

make	how	anywhere	which	wake up	dreams	everything	have to	will be	switch off

Welcome to my blog!

In 1949, George Orwell published his well-known novel *Nineteen Eighty-Four*. Now I, Megan Moore, will tell you my thoughts in a text entitled *Two Thousand Eighty-Four*. Hope you enjoy it and post your comments.

Two Thousand Eighty-Four

I guess things will be a lot different in 2084.
At school, we will sit on floating chairs and they will take us [1] ______________ we want to go. I think that we will have laptops built in our desks (no more pens or pencils) with a mini teacher inside and we will be able to [2] ______________ them ______________ when we get tired. That would be perfect!

At home, futuristic gadgets [3] ______________ everywhere. Housework will belong to domestic robots: we won't need to [4] ______________ our beds or clean the house. In our closets there will be intelligent clothes [5] ______________ will change color according to our mood and weather.

Thanks to nanotechnology, microcomputers will be implanted under our skin and any white wall will become a computer screen: you just [6] ______________ give a voice command: computer on! These computers will record [7] ______________ you see, eat, hear, say and do, even your [8] ______________ will be recorded. An alarm clock will [9] ______________ us ______________ for our morning appointments with the music of our preference playing inside our heads.

[10] ______________ about that?

Megan, 14, California

5 Answer the questions below based on the text in #4.

1 According to Megan, who will wash the dishes in the future?

____

2 What is special about the clothes we'll wear in the future?

____

3 Megan mentions George Orwell's book *Nineteen Eighty-Four*. What do **YOU** know about it?

____
____
____
____

6 Complete the sentences.

1 If I had a computer in my head,

______________________________.

2 If I could see my dreams as movies,

______________________________.

7 Which of Megan's ideas did YOU think was the most interesting? Why? Post your comments on Megan's ideas.

____
____
____
____
____

Want more?
Go to Word Log U8 (p. 100)

KEEPING YOUR ENGLISH UP OUTSIDE SCHOOL

1 **Look at the students below and what they do to improve their English when they are not at school. Check (✓) the strategies YOU too have used.**

2 **Think about the strategies YOU didn't check in #1. Why haven't you tried them? Which ones would you like to try?**

____

____

3 **Do YOU agree with the statements below? Write *yes* or *no* next to each sentence.**

1 Learning a foreign language doesn't happen only at school. ____________

2 I learn better when I'm on my own. ____________

3 I learn better practicing with friends. ____________

4 If I don't keep in contact somehow with the language, I end up forgetting it. ____________

5 It is important to practice my English outside school. ____________

6 It is easy to practice my English outside school. ____________

4 **What else can YOU do to improve your English?**

____

____

G1 Present perfect *vs.* Past simple

Present perfect	Past simple
I have lost my keys.	I lost my keys yesterday.
She has just left.	She left at 10 p.m.
Has he ever taken his MP4 player to class?	Did he take his MP4 player to class last week?

G1
I feel
:-D
:-)
:-/

1 Look at the G1 box. Circle the correct verbs below.

I [1] **didn't play / I've never played** soccer. I [2] **broke / have broken** my leg when I was little and I'm afraid I'll break it again. My friends [3] **didn't play / have played** all their lives, of course, but I don't like the sport. I [4] **always did / 've always done** lots of other sports like swimming, dancing and rock climbing. Last year I [5] **went / have been** to a camp and I learned to kayak. But really, I've never played soccer and I don't want to. It's too rough!

G2 Present perfect (aff., neg., int. + time expressions: *ever*, *never*, *already*, *yet*, *just*)

Affirmative	Negative	Interrogative
I have already been there.	We haven't visited Los Angeles yet.	Have you ever eaten Indian food?
He has just missed the bus.	She hasn't done the laundry yet.	Has it started yet?
They have never seen *Titanic*.		

G2
I feel
:-D
:-)
:-/

Attention: PRESENT PERFECT =
HAVE / HAS + PAST PARTICIPLE (reg. or irreg. verbs)

1 Look at the G2 box. Complete the sentences using the verbs in the *Present perfect* and the time expressions in parentheses.

1 ______________________ ? It's my favorite movie! (you / see / ever)
2 Kathleen and Bill ______________________ a new apartment. (find / just)
3 Nick and I ______________________ the test ______________ . (finish / yet)
4 Spencer ______________________ a foreign language. (study / never)
5 ______________ her music ______________ ? (hear / yet)

Grammar log Units 1 & 2

G3 Adverbs of manner & Comparative of adverbs

G3
I feel
:-D
:-)
:-/

Regular Adverbs	Irregular Adverbs
Mariah speaks slowly. = adj + -ly	fast ➜ fast good ➜ well hard ➜ hard early ➜ early late ➜ late
Martin and Sue laughed happily. = adj – -y + -ily	

Comparative Adverbs	
Jeff works more quietly than Stanley.	Please work harder. Shelton plays the guitar better than me.

1 **Look at the G3 boxes. Match the pictures with the sentences.**

[ ] Amy works hard.
[ ] Fred walks really fast.
[ ] She speaks French fluently.

1

2

3

2 **Look at the G3 boxes. Check (✓) the correct answers.**

1 Robert speaks	☐ more quickly than	☐ quickly	Phil does.
2 Jason runs	☐ faster	☐ faster than	on cold days.
3 Clarissa sings	☐ loudly	☐ more loudly than	most opera singers.

G4 Used to + infinitive (aff., neg., int.)

G4
I feel
:-D
:-)
:-/

Affirmative	Negative
Dennis used to study English two hours per day.	Mila didn't use to eat candy.
We used to travel to New York in the fall.	They didn't use to sing in public places.

Interrogative	Short Answers
Did you use to have long hair?	Yes, I did. / No, I didn't.
What did you use to do on cold days?	

1 Look at the G4 box. Check (✓) the correct sentence. Then correct the wrong one.

1 ☐ Mom and Dad used to spending a lot of money on Christmas shopping every year.

2 ☐ Dawson used to be a chubby boy, but he lost a lot of weight when he was eighteen.

____

G5 How long + Present perfect with *for* & *since*

G5
I feel
:-D
:-)
:-/

How long	has he worked as a biologist?	For ten years.
	have you had that car?	Since 2007.

1 Look at the G5 box. Unscramble the sentences and use the verbs in the correct form.

1 (be) / Brian and Julie / together / How long / ?

____

2 (be in love) / Gibson / since / with / Natalie / 1st grade / .

____

3 (live) / in Miami / three years / Chris and Max / more than / for / .

____

Unit 4

Grammar log

Grammar log Units 4 & 5

G6 Not as… as

G6 I feel :-D :-) :-/

Sentence	Meaning
Skateboarding is not as relaxing as sailing.	Sailing is more relaxing than skateboarding.
Chile and Argentina are not as big as Brazil.	Brazil is bigger than Chile and Argentina.

1 Look at the G6 box. Rewrite the sentences using *not as… as*.

1 My English is better than Matt's. ______________________

2 New York is noisier than San Francisco. ______________________

G7 Adjective + prepositions

G7 I feel :-D :-) :-/

fascinated by	responsible for	interested in	worried about	good at	afraid of	bad at

1 Look at the G7 box. Complete the sentences with *an adjective + a preposition*.

1 Marina is ______________ losing her job.

2 Why are you ______________ the dark?

3 A doctor is ______________ his patients' health.

4 Daniel is really ______________ drawing cartoons.

G8 What + look like? *vs.* What + be + like?

G8 I feel :-D :-) :-/

What + look like? *(appearance)*	What + be + like? *(personality)*
What does Ethan look like? He's tall and slim.	What is Olivia like? She's kind and friendly.
What do they look like? They are short and fat.	What are you like? I'm extroverted.

1 Look at the G8 box. Write questions for the following answers.

1 ______________________ She has black hair and green eyes.

2 ______________________ She's warm and witty.

3 ______________________ David's really sweet and intelligent.

G9 Relative clauses with *that, where, which & who*

G9
I feel
:-D
:-)
:-/

Who & that	I told you about that man. He is my neighbor.	➜	I told you about that man who / that is my neighbor.
Which & that	That is a CD. I like that CD very much.	➜	That is the CD which / that I like very much.
Where	This is a store. I bought my sunglasses here.	➜	This is the store where I bought my sunglasses.

1 Look at the G9 box. Fill in the blanks using the appropriate *relative pronoun*.

1 This is the supermarket ____________ caught on fire yesterday.
2 A factory is a place ____________ people produce things with the help of machines.
3 Do you know the guy ____________ is dancing with Sheila?
4 Who are you talking about? The boy ____________ is next to the teacher or the one ____________ is sitting behind Jessica?

G10 Pronouns: *one / ones*

G10
I feel
:-D
:-)
:-/

One ➜ Singular nouns	Ones ➜ Plural nouns
A The yellow T-shirt is cool.	A Those DVDs are fantastic.
B I prefer the black one. (= T-shirt)	B Which ones? (= DVDs)

1 Look at the G10 box. Circle the correct answers.

1 Which pants do you prefer: the blue **one / ones** or the green **one / ones**?
2 I would like to own a beautiful dress like this **one / ones**.
3 I love that blue T-shirt. Look... the **one / ones** on top of the pile.
4 The winner is the **one / ones** who gets here first.
5 A Where are may glasses?
B Which **ones / one**? The new **one / ones**?

Unit 5
Grammar log

G11 Pronouns: *some, any, no + one / body / thing / where*

	Affirmative	Negative / Interrogative	Negative
PEOPLE	Somebody / Someone has broken the window. I don't know who.	I didn't know anybody / anyone in that school.	No one / Nobody knows the correct answer.
THINGS	There's something in my eye.	Preston didn't say anything.	I know nothing about it!
PLACES	I've seen him somewhere before.	Do you live anywhere near here?	There is nowhere interesting to go.

G11
I feel
:-D
:-)
:-/

1 Look at the G11 box. Complete the following sentences.

1 I would like to go ______________ different on Saturday.
2 There wasn't ______________ there.
3 Look. There's ______________ to eat in the fridge. We have to go to the supermarket.

G12 Question tags

Affirmative sentences	Negative sentences
This is your street, isn't it?	That isn't your blouse, is it?
Shakira sings very well, doesn't she?	She doesn't know Pete, does she?
Maycon went to the movies with her, didn't he?	He didn't save money, did he?
You have chosen that dress, haven't you?	You have never traveled by plane before, have you?

Question tags and modals	
You can play the piano, can't you?	She can't sing, can she?
He should tell Mary, shouldn't he?	You shouldn't touch that, should you?
They could give us a prize, couldn't they?	We couldn't talk to our parents like that, could we?
I must lose some weight, mustn't I?	

G12
I feel
:-D
:-)
:-/

1 Look at the G12 box. Complete with the *Questions tags* and answers.

1 Mr. Dubois can't speak English, ______________ he? No, ______________ .
2 Tyler had a red car, ______________ he? Yes, ______________ .
3 Michelle has been to Los Angeles recently, ______________ she? No, ______________ .
4 We could have a party, ______________ we? Yes, ______________ .
5 We should buy the tickets now, ______________ we? Yes, ______________ .

G13 Possessive 's: singular & plural

G13 I feel :-D :-) :-/

Michael has a cap.	→	Michael's cap is blue and white.
Brandon and Kayla had an apartment in New York.	→	Brandon and Kayla's apartment was in Manhattan.
The Barkers had three cars.	→	The Barkers' cars were red, brown and black.
Justin and Lauren had different health problems.	→	Justin's and Lauren's health problems were different, but the same doctor treated them both.

1 Look at the G13 box. Write C for the *correct* sentences and W for the *wrong* ones. Then correct the *wrong* sentences.

1 Joseph and Grace's wedding was in Honey Beach. ☐ ____________________

2 Is that book yours or Sam? ☐ ____________________

3 Samantha's best friend went to Australia yesterday. ☐ ____________________

4 Nick and Amanda watches were stolen last week. ☐ ____________________

5 Billy's and Samuel's ball is in the yard. ☐ ____________________

G14 Present and past passive (aff., neg., int.)

G14 I feel :-D :-) :-/

Present passive	Past passive
The housework is done by Jessica.	The housework wasn't done yesterday.
Lunch is prepared.	Was lunch made by Mike?
The beds are made.	Were the beds made by Julie?

1 Look at the G14 box. Change the following sentences to the *Passive voice*. Decide whether to use *by* or not.

1 Did they close the store last Monday? ____________________

2 My dad photographed tigers in Asia. ____________________

3 People don't speak English in China. ____________________

4 The American chef George Crum invented the potato chips. ____________________

5 Fred gave Linda a car for her birthday. ____________________

G15 Going to & will

G15
I feel
:-D
:-)
:-/

We use *going to* and *will* to talk about things in the future. But what is the difference? Read the examples given and find out.

Amber *is going to* move to Canada in a few weeks. ➜ *Amber decided and planned to move <u>before now</u>.*

Really! I didn't know that. I*'ll* buy her a farewell present. ➜ *The speaker decided to buy her a present <u>now</u>.*

David, Leah and I *are going to* go dancing on Saturday. ➜ *The speaker decided and planned to go dancing <u>before now</u>.*

That sounds great! I*'ll* join you! Is that OK? ➜ *The speaker decided to go dancing <u>now</u>.*

1 Look at the G15 box. Use the verbs in parentheses to complete the sentences below.

1 Kim, are you having problems with your homework? I ____________ (help) you!
2 Jason and Nicole are excited about their trip next month to the USA. They ____________ (visit) New York, Miami and Orlando.
3 Look! That shop is on sale! I ____________ (buy) those jeans I told you about last week.

G16 Present continuous for future arrangements

G16
I feel
:-D
:-)
:-/

Affirmative	Negative	Interrogative
They *are flying* to Mexico next weekend.	Crystal *is not coming* on Friday.	What *are* you *doing* on Tuesday afternoon?

1 Look at the G16 box. Look at YOUR diary and write THREE sentences about arrangements you have for the week.

____
____
____
____
____
____

G17 Giving advice

G17
I feel
:-D
:-)
:-/

If I were you, I'd work less.
I wouldn't stop studying English if I were you
You ought to exercise every day.
You should drink more water.
You shouldn't eat so much junk food.

1 Look at the G17 box. Complete the sentences below.

1 That new coffee shop on Simms Street is great. The café latte is delicious! You ____________ try it!
2 I ____________ travel to the USA on vacation if I were you.
3 Linda, you ____________ eat so much candy. It's bad for your teeth.

G18 Second conditional: *If I* + past tense + *I would...*

G18
I feel
:-D
:-)
:-/

Attention We use **second conditional** sentences to talk about the things we imagine for the future.

If I won the lottery, I would travel around the world.
If you could have a beautiful mansion, where would it be?

1 Look at the G18 box. Complete the sentences using YOUR own words.

____________, I'd have breakfast in bed every day.

____________, I'd give a big party.

If I met Barak Obama, ____________

Unit 8

Grammar log

UNIT 1

Adjectives
embarrassing p. 10
outgoing p. 14
reasonable p. 14
rebellious p. 8

Job related words
a job interview p. 15
an application form p. 14
interests p. 15
relevant experience p. 15
salary p. 13
volunteers p. 14

Teen jobs
baby__________ p. 12
cleaning p. 12
dog w__________ p. 12
fast __________ work p. 12
homework __________ p. 12
household __________ p. 12
lawn __________ p. 12
newspaper __________ p. 12
pet __________ p. 12

Chunks
I don't recommend it. p. 10
It was awful! p. 10
It doesn't pay to (cheat)! p. 10
To change a diaper. p. 10
To have diaper rash. p. 10
To cheat on a test. p. 10
To invent a little white lie. p. 10
To make a long story short... p. 10
To be / get grounded. p. 10
Well, that depends. p. 13
Yes, lots of times! / loads of times! p. 11

UNIT 2

Everyday objects
a newspaper p. 22
a radio p. 22
a record player p. 22
an MP3 player p. 22

Newspaper sections
◯ Business p. 25
◯ Entertainment p. 25
◯ Fashion p. 25
◯ Gossip p. 25
◯ Home p. 25
◯ International p. 25
◯ Politics p. 25
◯ Science / Health p. 25
◯ Sport p. 25
◯ Travel p. 25

Things we wear
a mini-skirt p. 22
a tie p. 22
high-heeled shoes p. 22
reading glasses p. 22

Verb collocations
beg (for forgiveness) p. 20
break (a record, a leg) p. 23
catch (a criminal, a wild animal) p. 23
discover (a cure, some dinosaur bones) p. 23
elect (a new president, a leader) p. 23
get (married, divorced, better) p. 23
release (a new DVD, a film) p. 23
slam (the door) p. 20
win (an award, a medal, a competition) p. 23

Chunks
Can you believe it? p. 24
Congratulations! p. 19
Didn't you hear? p. 24
It's not fair. p. 21
There's none left! p. 19
You poor thing! p. 19

UNIT 3

Household appliances
a dishwasher p. 34
a fridge p. 34
a microwave oven p. 34
a radio p. 34
a sewing machine p. 34
a stove p. 34
a vacuum cleaner p. 34
a washing machine p. 34
an air conditioner p. 34

Chunks
◯ Are you serious? p. 32
◯ Let me have a look. p. 30
◯ No kidding! p. 30
◯ That's awesome! p. 32
◯ Unbelievable, isn't it? p. 32

>>

UNIT 4

Adjectives for describing jobs

badly-paid	p. 42
boring	p. 42
exciting	p. 42
interesting	p. 42
rewarding	p. 42
stressful	p. 42
tiring	p. 42
well-paid	p. 42

Occupations

a b___l___g___st	p. 42
a b___s___n___ss p___rs___n	p. 42
a d___v___r	p. 40
a l___wy___r	p. 42
a sc___nt___st	p. 42
a sh___rk k___p___r	p. 40
a t___r gu___d___	p. 44
an ___ng___n___r	p. 42
an ___T c___ns___lt___nt	p. 42

Places

a building site	p. 40
a slum	p. 38
an industry	p. 38
an office building	p. 40

Chunks

Money isn't everything!	p. 42

UNIT 5

Adjectives for describing people

◯ athletic	p. 48
◯ blond(e)	p. 48
◯ chubby	p. 48
◯ clever	p. 48
◯ cool	p. 48
◯ curly	p. 49
◯ cute	p. 49
◯ determined	p. 48
◯ easy-going	p. 48
◯ extroverted	p. 48
◯ funny	p. 48
◯ generous	p. 48
◯ good-looking	p. 49
◯ gorgeous	p. 48
◯ hairy	p. 49
◯ kind	p. 48
◯ serious	p. 49
◯ shy	p. 48
◯ slim	p. 48
◯ witty	p. 48

Clothes

baggy jeans	p. 54
designer clothes	p. 54
scruffy clothes	p. 54
tight jeans	p. 54

Magazine sections

Book / Movie reviews	p. 52
Health & Beauty	p. 52
Heroes	p. 52
Interviews	p. 52
Poetry	p. 52
Sports	p. 52
Travel and Culture	p. 52

Physical appearance

a body piercing	p. 54
a tattoo	p. 54
dyed hair	p. 54

Places

a library	p. 53
a stadium	p. 53
a supermarket	p. 53
an airport	p. 53
an arcade	p. 53

Chunks

Check it out!	p. 54
Which one / ones?	p. 55
Wow!	p. 49

UNIT 6

Collocations

be (__________, lost, __________)	p. 59
fail (a __________)	p. 59
lose (__________)	p. 59

Words related to sleeps & dreams

(be) asleep	p. 58
nightmares	p. 58
random images	p. 58
recurring dreams	p. 58

Chunks

Hang on a minute!	p. 59
It was absolutely disgusting!	p. 60
Last chance!	p. 59

Word log

UNIT 7

Computer technology

3D	p. 68
goods	p. 68
online community	p. 68
tools	p. 68

Things you don't know how to explain

alien	p. 74
enigma	p. 74
mystery	p. 74
puzzle	p. 74

Size

g__________	p. 74
h__________	p. 74
m__________	p. 74

Chunks

First of all...	p. 71
I don't think so.	p. 73
I think so.	p. 73
Who knows?	p. 74

UNIT 8

Household objects

[ ] air conditioner	p. 84
[ ] alarm clock	p. 84
[ ] faucet	p. 84
[ ] fridge	p. 84
[ ] mirror	p. 84

Chunks

Bye for now.	p. 80
I've got to go.	p. 78
I'm positive.	p. 78

WORLD ISSUES MAGAZINE

WI 1: The rights of children

Human rights related words

child labor
cruelty
freedom
housing
love
protection
recreation
tolerance

Expressions

to be (enslaved, recruited as soldiers, bused, trafficked, exposed to danger)
to labor on plantations
to mine precious metals
to pick over trash (in municipal dumps)
to work in factories

>>

WI 2: From generation to generation

Words & expressions related to stories

fairy tale
oral tradition
proverbs
Sufi stories

Chunks

Enjoy it!
To sleep like a log.
Wiser from the experience, wiser by the generation.

WI 3: Life matters

Life events

to get (your) first job
to get married
to go on (your) first date
to graduate from high school
to have (your) first child
to learn to read and write
to retire
to split up with someone
to start college
to turn 18

Chunks

For what it's worth...
Have the time of your life
Make the best of something

WI 4: Be what you wanna be

Occupations

computational linguist
image consultant
information broker
job developer
leisure consultant
myotherapist

Job related words / expressions

career opportunities
(professional) field
the fastest-growing occupations
to develop successful careers
to receive encouragement
work force
workplace

WI 5: Body image

Body reshaping

body piercing
bodybuilding
cosmetic surgeries
neck stretching
reconstructive surgeries

Eating disorders

anorexia
bulimia

WI 6: Sleeping like a log

Sleep related words & expressions
biological clock
feel sleepy
to sleep lightly
quality of sleep
to get sufficient sleep
to have sleep difficulties
to stay up late

Chunk
To make mistakes is human

WI 7: To believe or not to believe

ET related words & expressions
alien activity
humankind
mysterious epidemic

WI 8: What the future holds

Chunks
across the globe
for good
Go figure!
to keep up

>>

Irregular verbs

INFINITIVE	PAST TENSE	PAST PARTICIPLE
be born	was / were born	been born
be	was / were	been
become	became	become
break	broke	broken
bring	brought	brought
build	built	built
buy	bought	bought
choose	chose	chosen
come	came	come
cut	cut	cut
do	did	done
draw	drew	drawn
drive	drove	driven
eat	ate	eaten
fall	fell	fallen
feel	felt	felt
find	found	found
forget	forgot	forgotten
get	got	got
give	gave	given
go	went	gone (been)
grow up	grew up	grown up
have	had	had
hear	heard	heard
hide	hid	hidden

INFINITIVE	PAST TENSE	PAST PARTICIPLE
hit	hit	hit
know	knew	known
leave	left	left
lie	lay	lain
lose	lost	lost
make	made	made
meet	met	met
put	put	put
read	read	read
ride	rode	ridden
say	said	said
see	saw	seen
send	sent	sent
sleep	slept	slept
speak	spoke	spoken
take	took	taken
teach	taught	taught
tell	told	told
think	thought	thought
wake up	woke up	woken up
wear	wore	worn
win	won	won
write	wrote	written

Multi-word verbs

get back	get up	give up
go on	keep up	run out
switch off	work out	

Make & Do

MAKE	DO
a decision	a favor
a mess	business
a mistake	exercise
a phone call	good
an effort	harm
an exception	the homework

MAKE	DO
an excuse	the housework
arrangements	your best
money	
noise	
plans	

Track list

TRACK	PAGE	CONTENT
01	00	Introduction
02	07	Welcome Unit – L 2 – Ex. 3
03	08	U 1 – L 1 – Ex. 3
04	10	U 1 – L 2 – Ex. 1
05	12	U 1 – L 3 – Ex. 2
06	12	U 1 – L 3 – Ex. 4
07	14	U 1 – L 4 – Ex. 1
08	18	U 2 – L 1 – Ex. 3
09	20	U 2 – L 2 – Ex. 1
10	20	U 2 – L 2 – Ex. 3
11	24	U 2 – L 4 – Ex. 2
12	28	U 3 – L 1 – Ex. 1
13	30	U 3 – L 2 – Ex. 1
14	30	U 3 – L 2 – Ex. 3
15	32	U 3 – L 3 – Ex. 3
16	34	U 3 – L 4 – Ex. 1
17	38	U 4 – L 1 – Ex. 3
18	40	U 4 – L 2 – Ex. 2
19	42	U 4 – L 3 – Ex. 2
20	44	U 4 – L 4 – Ex. 2
21	49	U 5 – L 1 – Ex. 4
22	49	U 5 – L 1 – Ex. 5
23	50	U 5 – L 2 – Ex. 3
24	52	U 5 – L 3 – Ex. 1
25	54	U 5 – L 4 – Ex. 3
26	59	U 6 – L 1 – Ex. 4
27	60	U 6 – L 2 – Ex. 1
28	62	U 6 – L 3 – Ex. 1
29	62	U 6 – L 3 – Ex. 3
30	64	U 6 – L 4 – Ex. 1
31	68	U 7 – L 1 – Ex. 2
32	70	U 7 – L 2 – Ex. 2
33	72	U 7 – L 3 – Ex. 1
34	74	U 7 – L 4 – Ex. 1
35	78	U 8 – L 1 – Ex. 2
36	82	U 8 – L 3 – Ex. 3
37	84	U 8 – L 4 – Ex. 2

Name Class Date

1 Put the words in the correct order to make sentences in the *Present perfect*.

1 Japan / Hillary / never / to / been / has / .

Hillary has never been to Japan.

2 once / William / shaved / has / head / his / .

3 I / baseball / never / played / have / .

4 times / motorcycle / a / ridden / many / have / they / .

5 eaten / we / snails / have / never / .

2 Faith is talking about her family. Complete the sentences using the prompts below. Follow the example.

1 ✓ ride a camel
My aunt Marianne has ridden a camel ! She said it's a lot of fun!

2 ✗ go to the beach
My cousin Ken lives in the country and has never been to the beach . Can you believe that?

3 ✓ go to Disney World
My cousin Maggie ______ lots of times.

4 ✗ read a play by Shakespeare
My little brother is only 7! Of course he ______.

5 ✗ travel to Europe
My uncle John ______, but he dreams of going there one day.

6 ✓ jump out of planes
My dad's really brave. He ______ lots of times. He's a sky diver.

3 Fill in the blanks using the verbs in the box in the *Present perfect*.

dye be (2x) drive sleep

1 I have been to the hospital once.

2 Julia ______ her hair green! She looks really cool!

3 Paul's dad ______ a BMW! He said it's fantastic!

4 Gary and his friends ______ in a tent. Gary loved it, but his friends thought it was uncomfortable.

5 My best friend ______ to Japan. She doesn't like Japanese food, so she ate fast food every day.

4 What about YOU? Check (✓) the things you've done. Then write sentences.

- ◯ be abroad
- ◯ ride a horse
- ◯ eat sushi
- ◯ drive a car
- ◯ sleep in a sleeping bag
- ◯ dye my hair

1 I've been abroad. / I have never been abroad.
2 ______
3 ______
4 ______
5 ______
6 ______

1 Match the sentence halves to make questions.

1 Have you ever written [ ] frog's legs?
2 Have you ever ridden [ ] a camel?
3 Have you ever done [ ] a poem?
4 Have you ever sent [ ] an extreme sport?
5 Have you ever eaten [ ] an e-mail to a famous person?

2 Write YOUR answers to the questions in #1.

1 Yes, I've written a poem. / No, I've never written a poem.
2 ______
3 ______
4 ______
5 ______

3 Here are some more entries to the forum *PRESS THE REWIND BUTTON!* Read them and label the pictures with the nicks.

Message 1 posted by cutepatty yesterday

I went to a party in my sister's high-heeled shoes some months ago. Her feet are a bit bigger than mine, and as soon as I started dancing I tripped and fell down right in the middle of the dance floor! Everybody laughed at me. I just felt so ridiculous!

cutepatty

Message 2 posted by Baby_liz yesterday

I told my best friend I had a crush on a boy in our class. The next day the whole school knew about it and everybody teased me. I couldn't believe she did that to me! I never spoke to her again.

Baby_liz

Message 3 posted by sadrudy yesterday

Well, I liked a girl in my school and I thought she liked me too because she was always very friendly. So one day after school I asked her if she wanted to date me. She said "Sorry, Rudy, I already have a boyfriend". I was devastated!

sadrudy

4 What have the people in #3 learned? Write sentences using the verbs below.

find decide ask

1 Cutepatty ______ to wear shoes that fit her.
2 Baby Liz ______ a new best friend.
3 Sadrudy ______ out several girls but they all say no.

Name **Class** **Date**

1 **Circle the correct options to complete the sentences below.**

1 I think it's going to rain. You **should / mustn't** take an umbrella.
2 You **must / shouldn't** eat so much fast food. It's bad for you.
3 This is a no-smoking restaurant. **It's a good idea to / You mustn't** smoke in here.
4 When you surf the Web, **you should / it's not a good idea to** give personal information.
5 You **must never / should** forget to write your name when you do a test.

2 **Match the columns.**

1 You should exercise more.	[ ] You mustn't speak Portuguese.
2 This is an English class.	[ ] You should study more.
3 You didn't do well on your test.	[ ] I have a difficult test tomorrow.
4 I must study.	[ ] It's good for you.
5 The traffic light is green.	[ ] You mustn't cross the street.

3 **Here are some tips for students who want to get a job. Read the poster and write recommendations to a friend who is going to a job interview. Use different expressions:** ***must / mustn't / should / shouldn't / it's a good idea to / it's not a good idea to...***

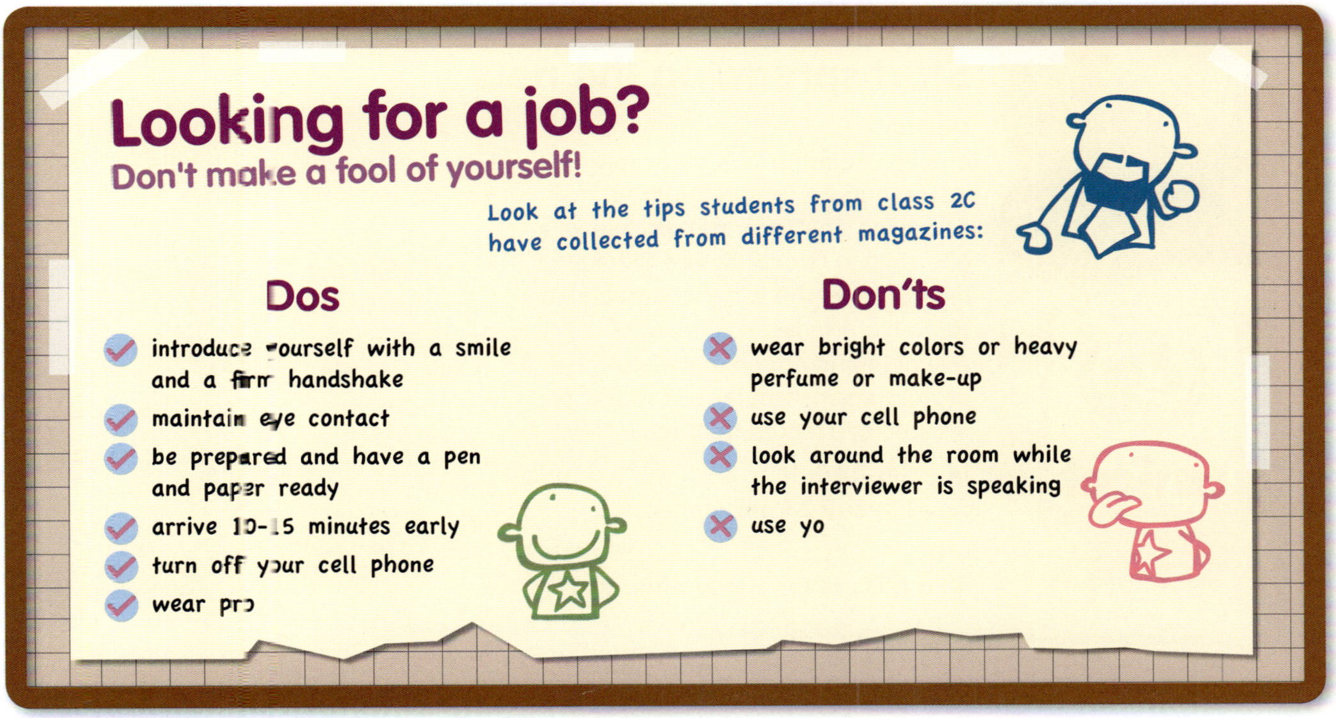

Example: You should introduce yourself with a smile and a firm handshake.

____

____

____

____

____

____

1 **Correct the sentences that are wrong. Check (✓) the ones that are right.**

1 ◯ Kelly arrived last Monday. ______
2 ◯ They have had lunch at 1 o'clock. ______
3 ◯ I've finished the exercise. ______
4 ◯ When have you traveled to the USA? ______
5 ◯ I didn't have time to do my homework yesterday. ______

2 **Write questions using the prompts below. Then answer them according to YOUR experiences. Follow the example.**

1 go abroad. *Have you ever been abroad? No, never. / Yes, I went to Chile last year.*
2 read a book in English ______
3 make a cake ______
4 break a mirror ______
5 tell white lie ______

3 **Read the following article from a magazine and complete it with the *Present perfect* or *Past simple* of the verbs in parentheses.**

Start spreading the nets

Malaria [1] ______ (be) a public health problem for many years in more than a hundred countries. In Africa, the disease kills one child in twenty before the age of five. But malaria is a preventable and treatable disease.
A simple and effective way to protect against malaria is to use of insecticide-treated bed nets (ITNs).

In 2006, UNICEF [2] ______ (buy) nearly 25 million nets.

UNICEF [3] ______ (help) fight malaria for a long time. It [4] ______ (distribute) ITNs for free to governments in malaria-endemic countries and [5] ______ (create) the "Spread the Net" campaign together with UNICEF Canada. In 2007, UNICEF and Canadian authorities proclaimed April 25 as Africa Malaria Day in Toronto. Since then they [6] ______ (work) to raise enough money to buy many more nets.

Adapted from: http://www.unicef.ca & www.malaria.org

4 **Answer the questions according to the article in #3.**

1 Is malaria a recent problem in African countries?

______

2 What is the simple way they found to protect people against malaria?

______

3 What has UNICEF done to help fight malaria?

______

Name Class Date

1 **Make sentences in *Present perfect* using the prompts below.**

1 she / read / that book She has read that book.
2 I / break / Mom's vase ______
3 he / make / a huge cake ______
4 we / not / finish / cleaning the house ______
5 Kate / not / open / her / present ______

2 **Read the sentences below. Write down the meaning of *'s*. Is it *is* or *has*?**

1 He's been here since 8 o'clock. has
2 She's a doctor. ______
3 She's lived in her present house for some months. ______
4 He's having dinner at the moment. ______
5 He's made a lot of money as an actor. ______

3 **Read the online article about the actress Drew Barrymore and complete the text with the verbs in parentheses. Use the *Present perfect*.**

Drew Barrymore [1] ______ (make) well-known movies such as *ET the Extra-Terrestrial*, *50 First Dates* and *Charlie's Angels*. In fact, she [2] ______ (be) an actress since she was 11 months old, when she made a food commercial. But success [3] ______ (not / come) easy. She started smoking cigarettes and drinking alcohol at a very early age. She also got involved with heavy drugs and went to a rehab center at the age of 13 for the first time. She [4] ______ (write) an autobiography, *Little Girl Lost*, where she talks about this troubled period of her life. Luckily, all this is behind her and now she is one of Hollywood's most successful stars.

Adapted from: http://en.wikipedia.org/

4 **Write about a movie YOU have seen. Say *when*, *where* and *who* you watched the movie with and give your opinion about it. Mention the items below.**

Title / Actors / The summary of the story

Example: I've seen many movies with Drew Barrymore but my favorite one was *Boys on the side* with Whoopi Goldberg and Mary-Louise Parker. It's a story about three friends. They are very different from each other but they are real friends. I watched this movie with my best friend some years ago. I really liked it. I think the story is beautiful and the actresses were great.

1 **Meg feels really happy when she thinks about her life. Write true sentences about Meg using *already* or *yet*. Use the prompts given.**

1 visit Paris ✓ Meg has already visited Paris.
2 graduate from university ✓ ______
3 get engaged ✓ ______
4 get married ✘ ______
5 have babies ✘ ______
6 buy apartment ✓ ______

2 **Write questions using the prompts. Add *yet* to the questions. Then answer them according to YOUR experiences.**

1 have lunch Have you had lunch yet? Yes, I have. / No, I haven't.
2 finish your math homework ______ ______
3 plan your weekend ______ ______
4 clean your room ______ ______

3 **Number the sentences to organize the dialogue below. Fill in the blanks with *already* or *yet*.**

Patrick

[1] So, Dad, is everything ready for the trip next Saturday?
[ ] OK, I'll do it now. You're always so disorganized, Dad.
[ ] To New York. And we haven't booked the hotel ______ . You know how crowded the city is this time of the year.
[ ] Dad! I can't believe it. You have ______ forgotten about the whole thing.

Mr. Owen

[2] The trip? Have we decided when we are leaving?
[ ] Oh, now I remember. Your Mom has ______ booked the rooms. But we haven't bought the tickets ______ . Could you do it?
[8] No, I'm not. I work too much. That's the problem.
[ ] Sorry, Patrick. We talked about so many things last week. Remind me, where are we going?

4 **Now write sentences about YOU. Say what you *have already done* today and what you *haven't done yet*.**

Example: I have already taken a shower. / I haven't taken a shower yet.

1 do homework ______
2 watch TV ______
3 have dinner ______
4 go to school ______

1 **Match the columns to form expressions.**

1 get	[ ]	a snack
2 win	[ ]	bad news
3 take	[ ]	from his bike
4 clean	[ ]	a shower
5 receive	[ ]	the kitchen
6 fall	[1/5]	a present
7 have	[ ]	the race

2 **Now use the expressions in #1 to say what has just happened in the pictures.**

1 Debbie has just won the race.

2 Lucy ____________________

3 Jacob ____________________

4 Alyssa ____________________

5 Dylan ____________________

6 Leah ____________________

7 The boys ____________________

3 **Read the dialogue below. Create a similar one.**

Kevin Let's go out, Wyatt.
Wyatt But I've just put my pajamas on!
Kevin Get changed!

1 **Complete the chart.**

INFINITIVE	PAST SIMPLE	PAST PARTICIPLE
be	was / were	been
________	had	had
know	knew	________
________	read	read
make	________	made
eat	ate	________

2 **Now complete the sentences below using some of the verbs from #1. Use the verbs in the correct tense. Use: *Present perfect*, *Past simple* or *Present continuous*.**

1 My aunt ________ to France many times. She loves it.
2 I'm not going to a restaurant now! I ________ just ________ dinner.
3 I ________ there was something wrong with him yesterday! He acted so strange.
4 I'm sorry. I can't help you now. I ________ the last pages of my book.
5 You ________ a big mistake last week when you left Alex alone.
6 ________ you ________ at that restaurant? It's really good.

3 **Now use the verbs in parentheses to complete the newspaper article. Use the *Present perfect*, *Past simple* or *Present continuous*.**

GAYS MILLS, Wis. (June 10) – For nearly a year, this small Wisconsin village [1] ________ (fight) against the most devastating force of nature: flooding. Floods [2] ________ (destroy) the town last weekend, forcing about 150 people to evacuate. Some families are waiting for good news about their missing relatives. The scenario is horrible. Firemen [3] ________ still ________ (try) to find survivors but there is little hope now. A team of engineers from the Wisconsin National Guard [4] ________ (work) at Lake Delton to determine which equipment is necessary to begin repairs on the homes that survived the flood.

Adapted from: http://news.aol.com/story/

4 **Complete the sentences about the village in #3.**

1 Last weekend, many families ________ (have) to fight against floodings.
2 A year ago, many people ________ (lose) their houses.
3 Now everything ________ (happen) again.
4 At the moment firemen ________ (work) to save more lives.
5 By now, over one hundred and fifty people ________ (leave) the town.

Name **Class** **Date**

1 **Complete the chart with the adverbs of manner. Circle the irregular adverbs.**

ADJECTIVE	ADVERB	ADJECTIVE	ADVERB	ADJECTIVE	ADVERB
fast	fast	slow		beautiful	
bad		good		late	
hard		careful		fluent	
easy		quiet		early	

2 **Now complete the sentences below using the verbs in parentheses and an adverb from #1. Pay attention to the verb tense you have to use.**

1 Nina ___speaks___ very ___quietly___ ! It's difficult to hear what she says. (speak)
2 Samuel ______________ for his tests. (study)
3 Of course my team won! We ______________ very ______________ ! (play)
4 We called the doctor and he ______________ . (arrive)
5 They ______________ ! They have wonderful voices! (sing)
6 I'm really tired today. I ______________ very ______________ this morning. (wake up)

3 **Look at the pictures. Write about them. Follow the model.**

Michael Phelps ______________
___swims fast / well___

Tortoises ______________
______________ .

Aaron Carter ______________
______________ .

Eagles ______________
______________ .

Yao Ming ______________
______________ .

Unscramble the letters to write the *adverbs of manner* in the comparative form.

1 tbetre – better
2 ileraer – ________
3 rdhare – ________
4 stfare – ________
5 rtlae – ________
6 fetibaluluy – more ________

2 Use the comparative form of the adverbs in #1 to complete the sentences below.

1 A Why did you arrive so early?
B Because I wanted to arrive ________ than the teacher and study a little more before the test starts.

2 A My dad has never had a car accident. He drives very well.
B Yes, but my uncle drives ________ than your dad.

3 A Sally can't run very fast. She has never won a race.
B You're right. Andrea and Polly can run ________ than Sally.

4 A I usually wake up late on Sundays, at about 10 or 11 a.m.
B But last Sunday I woke up ________ than you, at 11:30 a.m.!

5 A She dances beautifully.
B Yes, but when she was younger she danced even ________ .

3 Match the columns.

1 It's not fair! I studied harder than Joanna
2 "Don't use my MP4 player!"
3 If you continue practicing,
4 Hurry up!
5 Shhh! Don't speak so loudly!

[ ] you'll speak Spanish more fluently than Amelia.
[ ] You walk too slowly!
[1] and she got a better grade!
[ ] John said angrily to his little brother.
[ ] We're in a library!

4 Complete the following sentences. Give YOUR opinions using *adverbs of manner* in the comparative form.

1 I think Britney Spears sings ________ than Rihanna.
2 I usually wake up ________ than my parents.
3 I write ________ than my best friend.
4 I usually arrive in class ________ than the teacher.
5 I think the boys in my class speak ________ than the girls.

Name **Class** **Date**

1 Unscramble the sentences.

1 hair / Celia / to / have / used / long / . ______________________________
2 Pamela / play / sports / use / didn't / to / . ______________________________
3 thinner / used / be / to / Mrs. Smith / . ______________________________
4 glasses / didn't / wear / use / to / I / . ______________________________
5 used / big / in / we / live / to / a / house / . ______________________________

2 Complete the sentences about YOU. Use *used to* or *didn't use to*.

When I was a child I...

1 ______________________ play in the street.
2 ______________________ be afraid of the dark.
3 ______________________ believe in Santa Claus.
4 ______________________ visit my grandparents quite often.

3 Finish the sentences about the people in the pictures. Use *used to* in the affirmative or negative forms and the words in the box. Follow the model.

wear black clothes	wear glasses	
be friends	eat fruit	~~be fatter and shorter~~

1 Frank used to be fatter and shorter.

2 Three years ago Mr. Adams ______________________________

3 Lindsey ______________________________

4 Brandon and Nathan ______________________________

5 Natalie ______________________________

Match questions and answers.

1 Who did you use to play with? [ ] No, he didn't.
2 Did you use to have a lot of toys? [ ] I used to sit in front of the TV to relax a little.
3 Did your father use to wear glasses? [ ] Yes, we did.
4 Where did you use to play? [ ] My cousins and my friend Julianne.
5 What did you use to do after school? [ ] At my grandma's house. She had a big yard.

2 What about YOU? Answer questions 1, 2 and 4 in #1.

____

____

____

3 Write questions for the answers.

1 Did she use to have long hair?
Yes, she did, but now her hair is really short.

2 ____
No, they didn't. They used to go to school by bus.

3 ____
Yes, he did. He used to go to the movies every Saturday.

4 ____
No, she didn't. She used to study Spanish.

4 David is 15 and his mom asked him to do some housework before she left for work. Read the note David wrote, look at the pictures and write the missing words.

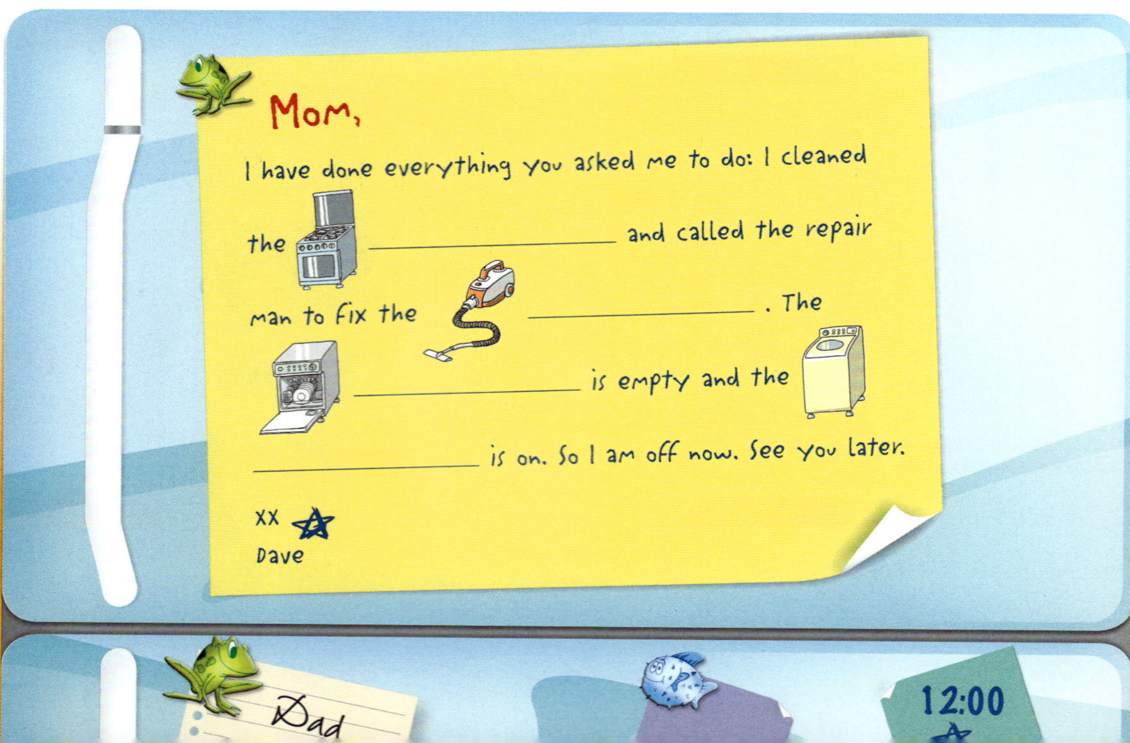

Name **Class** **Date**

1 **Match the columns.**

PLACES	CLUES
1 hospital	[ ] You find animals and plantations there.
2 farm	[ ] You find many workers and machines there.
3 slum	[ ] There are teachers and students there.
4 factory	[ ] Poor people in big cities live there.
5 school	[1] You go there when you have an accident.

2 **Look at the pictures. Complete the sentences using the *Present perfect*. Use the verbs in parentheses. Use *for* or *since* where necessary.**

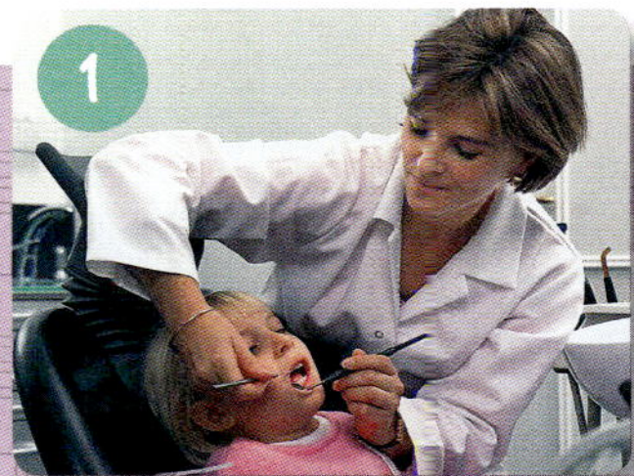

1 My mother ___has been___ (be) a dentist ___for___ 17 years.

2 The Walkers __________ (live) in the same house __________ their wedding.

3 They __________ (work) together __________ over a decade.

4 It __________ (rain) __________ March.

5 They __________ (fall) in love.

3 **Use the prompts and write true sentences about YOU. Use the Present perfect of the verbs and *for* or *since*.**

1 study / English I have studied English for two years.
2 study / at this school __________
3 have / a computer __________
4 live / in my house / apartment __________
5 know / my best friend __________

1 **Identify these people's occupations. Write the words.**

a sailor

____

____

____

____

____

____

____

2 **Where do some of the people in #1 work? Complete the sentences with the appropriate prepositions. Use *in* or *on*.**

1 Gardeners work ____in____ gardens.
2 Sailors work ______________ boats and ships.
3 Vets work ______________ clinics and ______________ farms.
4 Cooks work ______________ hotels, restaurants, etc.

3 **Unscramble the words to make questions with *how long*.**

1 have / long / how / been / you / in love How long have you been in love?
2 hairstyle / have / how / you / long / had / this ______________
3 have / known / you / your / how / long / teacher / English ______________
4 you / how / school / have / long / at / studied / this ______________

4 **Answer the questions in #3 about YOU. Use *for* or *since*.**

Example: I've been in love for 3 months. / I've been in love since last month. / (I'm not in love!)

1 ______________
2 ______________
3 ______________
4 ______________

Name Class Date

1 **Give YOUR opinion about the occupations below. Use the adjectives in the box or others you know.**

stressful	well-paid	interesting	exciting

1 doctor
I think doctors are well-paid, but it is a stressful job.

2 lawyer

3 IT consultant

4 athlete

2 **Now think of TWO occupations that relate to the adjectives listed below.**

1 tiring
2 badly-paid
3 rewarding
4 boring

3 **Use *not as... as* to change the sentences below.**

1 English is easier than Japanese.
Japanese isn't as easy as English.

2 Giovanni is taller than Mario.

3 Our dance teacher is older than our art teacher.

4 Surfing is more exciting than golf.

5 Pizza is better than lasagna.

4 **Think of people from YOUR family. What do they do? Compare their jobs using *(not) as... as*. Write TWO sentences.**

Example: My mother is a teacher and my father is a geologist. Working as a geologist is not as interesting as working as a teacher.

1
2

1 **Match the columns and check (✓) the correct option to make sentences.**

1 Our teacher is **interested**	[ ] **about** ( ) **travel** ( ) **traveling** without my baby brother.
2 I'm really **afraid**	[ ] **of** ( ) **ride horses**. ( ) **horses**. I fell off one when I was eight.
3 A firefighter is **responsible**	[ ] **by** ( ) **shoes and jewelry**. ( ) **buy shoes and jewelry**.
4 I'm not so **bad**	[ ] **at** ( ) **do tests**. ( ) **doing tests**. I got a B+ in science.
5 My parents are **worried**	[1] **in** (✓) **helping** ( ) **help** us with our composition.
6 In general, women are **fascinated**	[ ] **for** ( ) **saving** ( ) **save** people's lives.

2 **Now use the *adjectives + prepositions* in #1 to write sentences about YOU.**

Example: I'm interested in music and literature.

1 ______________________________

2 ______________________________

3 ______________________________

4 ______________________________

5 ______________________________

6 ______________________________

3 **Name the occupations below and say which one(s) YOU would like to have and why.**

____

____

____

____

____

____

Name **Class** **Date**

1 **Look at the pictures and check (✓) the correct answers to complete the dialogues.**

Dialogue 1

Jenny Paige, you have to meet my new boyfriend!
He's ◯ **gorgeous** ◯ **determined**!

Paige Really? ◯ **What does he look like?** ◯ **What's he like?**

Jenny He's blond and very ◯ **strong** ◯ **thin**.

Dialogue 2

Connor Hey, Mason. So you know that woman over there?

Mason Sure. She's my new art teacher.

Connor She's gorgeous! ◯ **What does she look like?** ◯ **What's she like?**

Mason Well, she's quite ◯ **funny** ◯ **boring**, actually. I nearly fall asleep during her lessons.

2 **Look at the pictures below. List FIVE adjectives YOU would use to describe these people.**

____

____

____

____

3 **Now read about the people in #2 and answer the questions.**

1 What does Jacob look like?

____

2 What is Jacob like?

____

3 What is Seung Eun like?

____

Jacob is a 25-year-old web designer. He is very young but he has had his own company for three years and makes presentations about web designing. He has lots of friends and enjoys telling jokes. He loves cycling and goes to work by bike every day. On the weekends, he goes out with his friends, goes cycling and swimming in the ocean.

Seung Eun was born in Korea but she has lived in New York since she was a baby. She is 23 now and a fashion designer. She decided to study fashion at a very early age and never gave up. She doesn't talk much but she has lots of friends who love being around her. She is always giving people advice on fashion and they love her brilliant ideas for clothes and accessories. Seung Eun has won a number of fashion competitions in the USA and abroad.

4 **What about YOU?**

1 What do you look like? What are you like?

____

Unit 5 - lesson 2

Workbook

1 **Read the article about Kat Von D. Fill in the blanks with *who* or *which*.**

SHE'LL GET UNDER YOUR SKIN

Have you ever heard of Kat Von D? She is the owner of a tattoo studio in LA and an artist [1] ___who___ is now in every newspaper and magazine. Her LA studio is a place [2] ________ offers something cool for every kind of person. In a city [3] ________ is famous for its tattoo culture, Kat Von D stars in a reality show called *LA Ink* [4] ________ promises to attract the attention of people from all over the world. But popularity and fame brings drama and hard work, too. Kat has a busy life and she has to coordinate a team of brilliant artists. And because they are all artists [5] ________ have their own personalities and strong opinions, the program is full of arguments and fun. Kat's TV program will show an LA [6] ________ is not commonly seen by outsiders.

Adapted from http://tlc.discovery.com

2 **Think of a TV show YOU love or hate. Circle the correct *relative pronoun* and complete the sentences below.**

1 It is a show **who / which** ________

2 My favorite character in the show is the one **who / which** ________

3 **Join the sentences using *who*, *which* or *that*.**

1 Pedro Bial is a TV host. He presents *Big Brother Brazil*.
Pedro Bial is the TV host who / that presents Big Brother Brazil.

2 *American Idol* is a reality show. It chooses the best singer in the USA.

____

3 Paula Abdul is a singer. She is one of the judges on *American Idol*.

____

4 *America's Next Top Model* is a TV show. It selects a top model from a large group of women.

____

4 **Do YOU like reality shows? Why?**

____

Name Class Date

1 **Look at the map below. Describe the places numbered in the map. Use *where*.**

1 The Peacefull Garden is the place where people can relax and watch the animals.

2 The Information Desk

3 The Princess Castle

4 Hungry Joey

5 Kids' Paradise

2 **Now think of TWO other places YOU would like to include in the park. Describe them.**

Example: The Arcade is the place where people can play electronic games.

1 ______

2 ______

3 **Use the phrases in the box and write about the places YOU usually go to.**

have fun	hang out	relax	swim	study	~~be alone~~

Example: My bedroom is the place where I go when I want to be alone.

1 ______

2 ______

3 ______

4 ______

5 ______

Unit 5 - lesson 3

Workbook

1 **Describe the people below. Say what they are wearing and mention particular features.**

Naomi

____
____
____
____
____
____

Grant

____
____
____
____
____
____

2 **Grant and Naomi are at the mall together. Complete the dialogue with *one* or *ones*.**

Grant So, Naomi, what exactly are we looking for?
Naomi I need a new pair of boots and I also want to buy my father a gift. Any ideas?
Grant What about a cap? Your dad goes jogging every day, right?
Naomi Great. A cap will do. What do you think of that [1] ______________ ?
Grant Are you serious? The orange [2] ______________ ? Oh, please, Naomi. Your dad would hate it. Get him the navy blue [3] ______________ .
Naomi OK, OK.
Grant Hey, what about those boots over there?
Naomi The black [4] ______________ ? No way! I want colorful boots, Grant.
Grant Colorful? You mean you like those pink [5] ______________ ?
Naomi Pink. Where? Oh, yes, that's what I mean. I'll take them.
Grant Oh, no!

3 **Which do YOU prefer? Answer using *one* or *ones*.**

1 Wich flip-flops do you prefer?

I prefer the black ones.

2 Wich backpack do you prefer?

____

3 Which dog do you prefer?

____

4 Which sunglasses do you prefer?

____

Name Class Date

1 **Read the following article about dreams. Complete the gaps with *somewhere*, *somebody / someone* or *something*.**

Ever wonder how you can interpret some of your dreams?

Chase dreams often represent feelings of anxiety in your life. Often in these dreams you are being chased by [1] ______________________ who wants to hurt or kill you. Then you run and hide [2] ______________________. It might indicate that you don't want to face your fears or a difficult situation in your life.

Flying dreams can have completely different meanings. If you are relaxed and having fun, then it suggests that you are on top of a situation. But if you have problems and feel afraid when you are flying, it represents [3] ______________________ which is standing in your way in life.

Now, when you wake up tomorrow, think about your dream and discover [4] ______________________ new about yourself!

Adapted from: http://www.dreammoods.com

2 **Read the article in #1 again. Answer the questions below.**

1 When you run from an attacker in a dream, what are you really running from in your life?

____

2 How can a person feel when dreaming about flying?

____

3 Have **YOU** ever had one of the dreams mentioned in the article? Do you agree with the interpretation in it?

____

3 **Answer about YOU.**

1 somewhere you like to stay:

____

2 someone you admire:

____

3 something you only wear at home:

____

4 something you enjoy eating:

____

5 someone you see every day:

____

6 somewhere you have been to:

____

1 Match the columns. Then give a true example about YOU for each item. Follow the model.

1 somewhere [ ] you can't live without.
2 someone [ ] you would like to visit.
3 something [ ] you've met recently.

Example: *Mexico is a place I'd like to visit. / Paulo Coelho is someone I… / My MP4 player is something I…*

1 ______________________________
2 ______________________________
3 ______________________________

2 Josh is 14 and has lots of questions on his mind. Complete the paragraph with *any / some / no + thing / body / where.*

I have no idea what I want to do with my life. I'd definitely like to live [1] ____________ abroad, but I'm not sure where. It could be [2] ____________ , really. I just want to live in a different country. And I guess I'll get married some day, but I won't meet [3] ____________ interesting at my school. I need a change. I've already told Mom that! There's [4] ____________ I can do without her permission. I hate to be 14. I'd like to have [5] ____________ to talk to and get advice from, but I can't talk to [6] ____________ at home. They never seem to understand me. I hope [7] ____________ good happens in my life!

3 Josh plays the guitar and writes songs. These are the lyrics he wrote for a new song. What are the missing words? Choose the correct options.

I don't do [1] ____________
I don't talk to [2] ____________
I don't go [3] ____________

My life has stopped
And I desperately need some air.

I'll find [4] ____________ to love
I'll find [5] ____________ to go
[6] ____________ can stop me
From knowing what I know

1	(a) something	(b) nothing	(c) anything
2	(a) somebody	(b) nobody	(c) anybody
3	(a) somewhere	(b) nowhere	(c) anywhere
4	(a) someone	(b) no one	(c) anyone
5	(a) somewhere	(b) nowhere	(c) anywhere
6	(a) Something	(b) Nothing	(c) Anything

Name Class Date

1 **Josh really wants to change things in his life. Read this conversation with his therapist and complete the dialogue using the appropriate *question tags*.**

Dr. Kane So, Josh. You're having problems at school, [1] ________________ ?

Josh Yeah, well, could we talk about something different today, Dr. Kane?

Dr. Kane Sure. What do you want to talk about?

Josh I want to change things in my life. For real, this time.

Dr. Kane Hum... interesting. You want to go to a different school, [2] ________________ ?

Josh Yes, but Mom won't let me. And I'll never meet any nice girls where I am now.

Dr. Kane Oh, girls. The girls from your school don't talk to you, [3] ________________ ?

Josh They're stupid. And I don't like them anyway. And I'm also mad about my semester abroad. Mom promised me I would go abroad for a semester, and now...

Dr. Kane But you aren't 16 yet, [4] ________________ ? I remember she said 16...

Josh I can't understand why I have to wait for two years. I could go now, [5] ________________ ? I already know where I want to go.

Dr. Kane Well, let's talk about school, Josh. Tell me. You missed some classes last week, [6] ________________ ?

Josh But I don't want to talk about that!

2 **Would YOUR parents allow you to study abroad? If so, where would you like to go? Why?**

____

3 **Josh had a weird dream last night. His therapist wants to know more about it. Put the words in order to find out the questions Dr. Kane asked Josh. Complete the questions with a suitable *question tag*. Follow the model.**

1 weren't / you / alone
You weren't alone, were you?

2 people's / see / you / didn't / faces
____

3 you / something / found
____

4 afraid of / you / it / were
____

5 before / you / that / have had / dream
____

1 **What do YOU know about Indira Gandhi? Read her biography and answer the questions.**

Born in India, Indira Gandhi spent part of her childhood in Allahabad, India, where her family had its family home. She received her college education at Somerville College in Oxford, England.
Indira Gandhi served as India's Prime Minister from 1966 to 1977, but she lost the 1977 election. However, in 1980, she was re-elected to the position.
She established ties with the Soviet Union early in the 1980's, but then got closer to the United States and the West. In 1984 Gandhi ordered an attack on nationalist extremists. In response to this attack, Gandhi was assassinated by one of her own guards on October 31, 1984.
Indira Gandhi had no direct relationship to Mahatma Gandhi. He was only a family friend. Both of them had major roles in Indian politics, and they both died for their political views and attitudes.

Adapted from www.wikipedia.com

1 Where was Indira from? ____________________
2 Where did she graduate from college? ____________________
3 When did Indira return to the position of Prime Minister? ____________
4 Who killed her? ____________________
5 Why was she killed? ____________________
6 Were Indira and Mahatma Gandhi relatives? ____________________

2 **Here are some other facts about Indira's life. Rewrite the sentences using the *possessive 's*.**

1 Indira had a husband, Feroze, but he died in 1960.
Indira's husband died in 1960.

2 Indira was the only child her parents had.
Indira was ____________ only child.

3 Indira had two sons and both of them followed her career.
____________ sons followed her career.

4 Indira and Feroze had a son, Rajiv, who became the Prime Minister after Indira's death.
____________ son became the Prime Minister after ____________ death.

5 Indira and Mahatma had different beliefs but they both worked hard till they died.
____________ beliefs were different but they both worked very hard till they died.

3 **What does the *'s* stand for in the following sentences? *Is*, *has* or the *possessive 's*?**

1 Nate**'s** coming for dinner tonight.
is

2 Sandra**'s** best friend arrived from Miami yesterday.
____

3 She**'s** just called and left a message.
____

4 I guess Brianna**'s** not happy at her new school.
____

5 Here**'s** my ball. Oh, no! It**'s** broken Mom**'s** vase.
____
____
____

Name Class Date

1 Use the verbs in parentheses in the *Passive voice* to complete the ad about a new computer game called *RollerCoasterXtreme*.

Imagine an amusement park you can go to every day if you want. Try *RollerCoasterXtreme*! When you play *RollerCoasterXtreme* you not only feel you are at an amusement park, but you also feel in control of it! Rides [1] ____________ (build) when and where you decide. Roller coasters [2] ____________ (design) according to your choices and desire. Workers [3] ____________ (hire) depending on your opinion and even prices [4] ____________ (set) by you! Remember, guests [5] ____________ (keep) happy if you are a good manager. If not, you might have problems! Take a free ride and become a *RollerCoasterXtreme* manager. Have fun!

2 Use the prompts to write sentences about other features of *RollerCoasterXtreme*.

1 Park employees / monitor / 24 hours a day / .
Park employees are monitored 24 hours a day.

2 Rides / check / every day / .
____

3 The park / clean / every hour / .
____

4 The park / protect / from vandalism / .
____

3 These are the steps you have to follow to create your own roller coaster. Use the prompts to write the sentences. Then number the steps in the correct order.

track / build

engine / install

cars / choose

roller coaster / test

[1] The track is built.
[ ] ____________
[ ] ____________
[ ] ____________

4 Do **YOU** like amusement parks? Answer the questions below.

1 Have you ever been to an amusement park? What was it like? Where was it?
____

2 If not, would you like to go to one? Why?
____

3 What is the best thing about amusement parks?
____

1 **Do *YOU* have a blog? Do you read blogs? What are the blogs you read?**

____

____

2 **The following questions are in the list of *Frequently Asked Questions* (FAQs) at *www.bloggerforum.com*. Complete them with the *Passive form* of the verbs in parentheses.**

1 Where ______________ my blog ______________ (host)?
2 How ______________ the original template ______________ (edit)?
3 How ______________ special characters and symbols ______________ (add)?

3 **Now match these answers to the questions in #2.**

[ ] There are a few HTML tips and tricks for adding them.
[ ] *Blogger* can give you free hosting on *Blogspot*.
[ ] You should go to your "Templates" tab.

4 **This is a list of other guidelines for people who want to have their own blogs. Rewrite the sentences using the *Passive voice*.**

1 Moderators choose the "Blog of the Week" based on content and design.
The "Blog of the Week" is ______________________________

2 They post blogs that join the forum in the Hot Links list.
Blogs that join the forum ______________________________

3 Some firewall systems block the *Blogger* page.
The *Blogger* page ______________________________

5 **Give short answers to the questions below based on the information in #3 and #4.**

1 Are blogs hosted on *Blogspot*?
____

2 Are all blogs posted in the Hot Links list?
____

3 Is the *Blogger* page blocked by some firewall systems?
____

4 Do moderators look at design when they vote for the "Blog of the Week"?
____

Name Class Date

1 **Do YOU know what *Havaianas*® are and how they became the success they are today? Read the magazine article below and find out more about Brazil's most famous footwear.**

It was in 1962 that it all started to come true. The Japanese Zori flip-flop sandals inspired *Havaianas*®: Brazilian flip-flops made of rubber and 100% made in Brazil. They were a durable, comfortable and inexpensive product. Two years later, producers named these rubber flip-flops *Havaianas*® and stores sold about 1,000 pairs a day. In 1970, they produced a publicity campaign starring the famous actor and comedian Chico Anysio. They wanted to differentiate the *Havaianas*® from imitations around the country. At that time, *Havaianas*® were not so popular among teenagers and people from upper classes. In 1994, *Havaianas*® *Top* were launched: they were a single color sandals that became everyone's favorite. They were comfortable, cheap and cool to wear! After that, things never stopped getting better. In 2000, paparazzi photographed top models wearing *Havaianas*® and the company exported more and more sandals. Think about how many pairs you have, and also about how many pairs you would like to have! Maybe that's why *Havaianas*® is such a good business!

Adapted from: http://www.havaianas.com.br/eng/1024/home.html

2 **Answer the questions based on the article in #1.**

1 How long has *Havaianas*® had its name? ______

2 When did *Havaianas*® become popular among people of all ages and social classes? ______

3 Why do **YOU** think there were imitations of *Havaianas*® on the market? ______

3 **These are sentences from the article in #1. Rewrite them using the *Passive voice*.**

1 The Japanese Zori flip-flop sandals inspired *Havaianas*®.
Havaianas® were inspired by the Japanese Zori flip-flop sandals.

2 Producers named these rubber flip-flops *Havaianas*®.
______

3 Stores sold about 1,000 pairs a day.
______

4 In 1970, they produced a publicity campaign.
______

5 In 1994 they launched *Havaianas*® *Top*.
______

6 In 2000, paparazzi photographed top models wearing *Havaianas*®.
______

4 **What is YOUR opinion about these flip-flops?**

______

1 **Have YOU heard of Machu Picchu? What do you know about it? Read this travel brochure and learn more about Machu Picchu. Complete the text with the phrases from the box and with the *Passive form* of the verbs in parentheses.**

by the Spanish | by the Incas | by smallpox

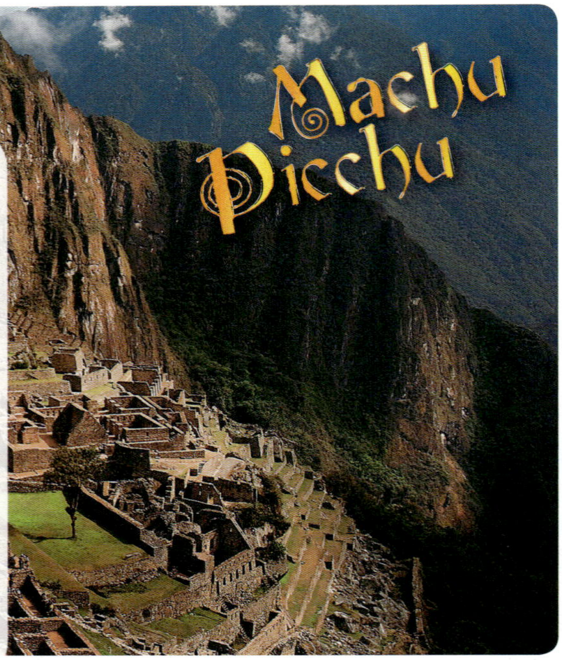

Machu Picchu is probably the most well-known symbol of the Inca Empire. Machu Picchu [1] was constructed (construct) around 1460 [2] ____________. It [3] ____________ (abandon) less than 100 years later, when most of the people living there were killed [4] ____________.
Apparently, the Machu Picchu area [5] ____________ (choose) carefully. It [6] ____________ (build) about 80 kilometers from Cusco, the Inca capital, but it [7] ____________ (never / find) and consequently, not destroyed [8] ____________.
The Machu Picchu ruins are there to tell us a story.
Nowadays, Machu Picchu is one of the most popular tourist sites in South America, visited by over 400,000 people every year.

Adapted from: http://en.wikipedia.org

2 **Answer T for *true* or F for *false*.**

Vocabulary Box
Smallpox is an infectious disease also known by the Latin names **Variola** or **Variola vera**.

1 [ ] Machu Picchu was a city built by the Incas.
2 [ ] Machu Picchu was built near Cusco.
3 [ ] Many inhabitants of Machu Picchu were killed by an infectious disease.
4 [ ] Machu Picchu was destroyed by the Spanish.

3 **Would YOU like to visit Machu Picchu? Why?**

____

4 **Read the newspaper headlines and check (✓) the ones where the *by* phrase can be omitted.**

- The ruins of Machu Picchu were rediscovered in 1911 by Yale archeologist Hiram Bingham ☐
- Hundreds of people killed by smallpox in Eastern Africa ☐
- Baby saved by a 13-year-old boy ☐
- National bank was robbed by thieves last night ☐
- An Olympic Gold Medal was won by a young Brazilian swimmer ☐
- Walls built by workers in Beijing to hide ugly buildings ☐
- Famous painting stolen yesterday by museum security guard ☐

1 **Akira and Kirsten are on their fifth date. Complete their conversation with *will* or *going to* and the verbs in parentheses.**

Kirsten This is a cool restaurant, Akira.

Akira Yeah, I think so too. And everything here is just delicious. Let me see, I [1] ______________ (have) a double cheeseburger, French fries and diet soda. And vanilla ice cream for dessert! What about you?

Kirsten Well, I can't eat that much. I [2] ______________ (play) volleyball, remember? And it's an important game for us. We have to win! I guess I [3] ______________ (order) a strawberry smoothie.

Akira Their smoothies are great! I'm sure you [4] ______________ (love) it. So, what about the game?

Kirsten Well, it's the most important game of the season for us. We've talked about it all week. And we're a bit nervous. Everybody [5] ______________ (be) there, you know.

Akira Relax, Kirsten. You [6] ______________ (be) fine. So, [7] ______________ we ______________ (see) each other after the game? We could go to the movies or something.

Kirsten Sure! But only if we win, Akira. If they beat us, I [8] ______________ (stay) with the team to talk the game over – coach's orders.

2 **What do YOU usually order when you go to your favorite snack bar?**

____

3 **Imagine the scenarios below. For each one, imagine Kirsten's plans.**

1 Kirsten couldn't be any happier. Her team won the game and she went out with Akira. Now she is at home thinking about what she plans to do tomorrow.

____

2 Kirsten doesn't feel well. Her team lost the game and the coach made them stay at school and analyze the game for hours. She didn't see Akira and she feels sick. Now she is at home thinking about what she plans to do tomorrow.

____

Workbook Unit 8 - lesson 2

1 **Complete the phrases with *make* or *do*.**

1 make a decision
2 ________ your best
3 ________ a favor
4 ________ a mistake
5 ________ plans
6 ________ business
7 ________ a phone call
8 ________ arrangements
9 ________ your homework
10 ________ the housework

2 **Use the phrases in #1 to answer the questions below.**

What do **YOU** do when...

1 ... you want to choose what clothes to wear? I make a decision.
2 ... you want to meet a friend during the weekend? ________
3 ... you help your mom at home? ________
4 ... you want to impress someone? ________

3 **Look at Olivia's diary for the next few days. Complete the dialogue below. Use *the Present continuous* of the verbs in parentheses to talk about future arrangements.**

WEDNESDAY	THURSDAY	FRIDAY	SATURDAY
1 p.m. lunch with Michael	3 p.m. doctor	9 a.m. dentist	12:30 lunch at Uncle Jerry's
4 p.m. 1st yoga class (cancelled ☹)!	6 p.m. meet Vanessa / movie	5 p.m. Mom's birthday present	2 p.m. see Grandma

Olivia Hello.
Eric Hi, Olivia. It's me, Eric.
Olivia Eric? Oh, Eric! It's been ages!
Eric I know! Listen, I want to see you. This school break is a good opportunity. Let's get together some day this week.
Olivia OK. What do you have in mind?
Eric What about lunch today?
Olivia I [1] ________ (have) lunch with a friend to discuss some private stuff, so I can't invite you to join us. Sorry.
Eric No problem. What about an ice cream or something in the afternoon?
Olivia I [2] ________ (start) my yoga classes today at 4, and I can't miss it!
Eric Oh, OK. Tomorrow then?
Olivia Tomorrow is a busy day, Eric. I [3] ________ (see) the doctor at 3 and then Vanessa and I [4] ________ (meet) at the mall. We [5] ________ (catch) a movie.
Eric Vanessa! Nice. Perhaps I could join you.
Olivia Well, I don't think it is a good idea. We chose a silly girly movie. And Friday isn't such a good day, either. I [6] ________ (go) to the dentist's in the morning and in the afternoon I have to go shopping.
Eric So Saturday will be our day!
Olivia No chances on Saturday either: I [7] ________ (eat) lunch at a new restaurant in town with my uncle. Then we [8] ________ (visit) grandma. And I'm seeing my boyfriend after that. Listen, Eric, I am sorry.
Eric Your boyfriend? Oh, that's fine. OK. No problem. Bye.

Name **Class** **Date**

1 **Read the e-mails below. They were sent to Hannah Owen, a 16-year-old American girl who has a problem page in *US Teen*. Fill in the gaps with the appropriate *multi-word verb* in the correct tense. There is an extra verb which will not be used.**

run out   switch off   give up   work out

Hey, Hannah.
How r u?
I'm kind of in love with a girl so I tried to ask her out, but I think she just gave me lots of excuses about why she couldn't go out. And I'm sure she invented a boyfriend!
My friends have told me to ________________ , but I'm not sure I should. What do you think?
Eric

Dear Hannah,
My older brother is driving me crazy! He ________________ at home every day and uses my MP3 player to listen to music while he exercises. The problem is he never returns it. What can I do?
BFN,
Lizz

Dear Hannah,
My mom insists I play the piano but I hate it! 2nite I'm having my first piano lesson and I've ________________ of excuses not to go. Help me, please!
Thanks,
Becca

2 **The following sentences were taken from Hannah's answers. Who received each piece of advice? Write E (Eric), L (Lizz) or B (Becca) next to each sentence.**

1 [ ] You ought to make her listen to you.
2 [ ] If I were you, I'd be really direct and tell her how you feel.
3 [ ] Before going on, you should try to find out if she really has a boyfriend or not.
4 [ ] You ought to try to talk to him about it.
5 [ ] You should hide your things from him.
6 [ ] You shouldn't lie or make up excuses. Tell the truth.

3 **Look at Hannah's advice in #2. Rewrite the sentences using the words in parentheses.**

1 (should) You should make her listen to you.
2 (ought to) You ________________
3 (if) ______ I were you, I would ________________
4 (if) ________________
5 (shouldn't) ________________
6 (if) ________________

4 **If YOU were in Hannah's shoes, what extra piece of advice would you give? Write a sentence for each person.**

1 Eric ________________
2 Lizz ________________
3 Becca: ________________

1 **Matt is 16 years old and it is his school break now. Look at his thoughts and complete the sentences. Use the prompts in parentheses**

1 (be 18 – be able to go to concerts)
If I were 18 years old, ______________________________

2 (not have a little sister – watch stupid things on TV)
____

3 (have enough money – buy that cap)
____

2 **Now talk about YOU. Complete the sentences below.**

1 If I had more free time, ______________________________
2 If I lived alone, ______________________________
3 If I had to change schools, ______________________________
4 If I found $100 in the street, ______________________________

3 **Circle SIX items you can find in a home.**

A	S	G	Y	H	N	U	C	M	I	P
I	L	J	E	W	O	Q	S	I	B	B
R	Z	T	V	E	I	M	X	R	P	L
C	O	E	F	O	G	T	R	R	V	I
O	A	L	A	R	M	C	L	O	C	K
N	N	E	U	H	I	A	A	R	P	E
D	B	V	C	J	C	R	E	I	P	L
I	I	I	E	B	G	R	S	D	H	J
T	O	S	T	A	S	V	R	R	M	I
I	Y	I	W	K	F	O	I	L	E	A
O	P	O	C	U	W	R	J	A	Y	V
N	T	N	I	A	E	B	I	N	U	N
E	K	Y	T	H	C	W	X	D	U	O
R	E	E	H	T	U	Y	L	I	G	A
A	I	I	C	O	N	R	I	T	I	E

4 **Now choose THREE items from #3 and define them. Follow the example.**

Example: Fridge – It's something which we use to keep food cool.

1 ______________________________
____
____

2 ______________________________
____
____

3 ______________________________
____
____